Decision-Making by the Book

Discovery House Publishers

Books, music, and videos that feed the soul with the Word of God

Box 3566 Grand Rapids, MI 49501

Decision Making by the Book

How to Choose Wisely in an Age of Options

Discovery House Publishers is affiliated with RBC Ministries, Grand Rapids, Michigan 49512.

Discovery House books are distributed to the trade exclusively by Barbour Publishing, Inc., Uhrichsville, Ohio 44683.

Library of Congress Cataloging-in-Publication Data

Robinson, Haddon W.
    Decision-making by the Book : how to choose wisely in an age of options / Haddon Robinson.
      p.   cm.
    Originally published: Wheaton, Ill. : Victor Books, © 1991.
    ISBN 1-57293-021-7
    1. Decision-making—Religious aspects—Christianity. 2. Christian life.
I. Title.
[BV4509.5.R63   1997]
248.4—dc21   97-4944
                                                    CIP

Printed in the United States of America

02 03
/ CHG /
3 5 7 9 10 8 6 4

Contents

Dedication

To my three associates in ministry
Nancy Hardin
Alice Mathews
Lori Seath
who have consistently stifled my creativity by insisting that a word can be spelled only one way.

Acknowledgments

I acknowledge my debt

• To the members of the men's Bible study in Denver. They encouraged me to teach on decision-making and told me they found the lessons helpful.

• To Steve Rabey, who edited the transcripts and pressured me to finish the manuscript.

• To Phil Murdy and Rebecca Thompson, who lent their energy to the finished product.

• To the faculty, administration, and staff of Denver Seminary, who have helped me learn about decision-making the hard way—by correcting the bad ones and carrying out the good ones.

Introduction

A reporter investigating the citrus industry in Florida went into a shed where he saw a man sorting oranges. As the oranges came tumbling down the conveyer belt, the man went to work putting the large oranges in the large holes, the small oranges in the small holes, and the bruised oranges in another hole.

The reporter watched this man perform his incredibly boring job until he couldn't stand it any longer. Finally, he asked the man, "Doesn't it get to you? I mean, how can you stand putting those oranges into those holes all day long?"

"You don't know the half of it," said the man. "From the time I come in until the time I leave, it's decisions, decisions, decisions!"

That man with his oranges illustrates an important point: Life is made up of decisions. Some decisions are small, some are large. But from beginning to end, it seems that life is nothing but decisions, decisions, decisions.

We have to decide whether we're going to get up in the morning. Having made that major decision, we decide what to have for breakfast. Next we must decide what to wear for the day. Before we know it, we have to decide what to have for lunch. After lunch, we decide what we're going to do in the afternoon. The evening brings decisions of whether or not we're going to watch television and if so, what to watch. Finally, we decide when to go to bed, and whether to have cookies and milk before turning in.

Big Choices in Tough Times

Most of us handle these routine decisions with relative ease. But life often presents us with many larger decisions that confront and confuse us. These are the big, crucial decisions which, when we make them, turn around and make us. These decisions begin in our teens when we decide what we want to do when we grow up. We have to decide whether or not to attend college. If we go, which courses will we take and what will be our major? After graduation, we must decide whether to take a job or go to graduate school. And along the way we may have to decide whether or not to marry and who the lucky someone will be.

Had we lived during the eighteenth century, some of these decisions might have been easier than they are today. The son of a blacksmith would likely follow in his father's trade. A daughter would bear the responsibilities of the home, as her mother and grandmother before her. Our world would consist of a small community and a few nearby towns, allowing us a limited number of prospective mates.

Today things are much different. Occupations are much more specialized. Choosing a vocation and deciding how to prepare for it seem much more complex than they were centuries ago. And thanks to technologies like the telephone and the airplane, which allow us to cross oceans in just minutes or hours, today's men and women may meet hundreds—perhaps thousands—of people every year.

It was 1970 when Alvin Toffler wrote *Future Shock*. In that watershed book, Toffler gave us a word for the malaise that many of us have already acknowledged—overchoice. We can see examples of overchoice everywhere—on our TVs, where dozens of cable channels compete for our attention, and on the shelves of our supermarkets, where dozens of dry cereals vie for our dollar.

In one of his most poignant examples, Toffler cited a study of overchoice in the automobile market. A computer specialist sat down at a computer and entered all of the variations available in automobiles—body styles, colors, accessories. After the computer groaned and blinked for a few seconds, it revealed this startling finding: American consumers could choose from some 25 million different automobiles. And selecting a car is a relatively easy decision!

Not only are we trying to make tough decisions in the midst of amazing complexity, but we're also hearing more and more about how important our decisions are and how far-reaching their consequences can be. Men and women in our society face critical choices on issues as diverse as abortion, Third World starvation, nuclear war, the environment, and genetic engineering. Increasingly, our decisions have ripple effects that extend far beyond ourselves to an unborn child, our family, our church, or even our world.

A Hunger for Guidance

I speak at scores of conferences, churches, and seminars each year. And one question people ask me over and over is, "How can I know the will of God?"

With all of life's complexities, pressures, and decisions, it's no wonder that people are concerned. We would like a telephone hot line directly to God's throne. That way, we could know God's will on everything from what career to pursue to what shoes to wear.

Unfortunately, many people let their hunger for guidance lead them into dangerous ways of seeking God's will. In this book we'll examine what God says about guidance and decision-making. Along the way we may find a few surprises as we take a look at some of the poorer methods we have used to make decisions. Hopefully, in the end, we'll have a much clearer picture of how we can make choice choices.

1

Looking for the Will of God

"Let no one be found among you who sacrifices his son or daughter in the fire, who practices divination or sorcery, interprets omens, engages in witchcraft, or casts spells, or who is a medium or spiritist or who consults the dead. Anyone who does these things is detestable to the LORD, and because of these detestable practices, the LORD your God will drive out those nations before you."

(Deuteronomy 18:10–12)

People have devised all kinds of approaches in seeking God's will. Some consult Ouiji boards. Some go to New Age "channelers," who claim to be the vehicles for the counsel of wise people long dead. Some flip a coin. And some sophisticated church leaders use computer-generated probability studies. They argue that it's God's will to use technology to seek God's will.

But seeking God's will didn't begin in the twentieth century. As far back as we can go in recorded history, people have tried to get divine guidance for the living of life.

Among followers of the ancient pagan religions, knowing the mind of the gods was a central concern. Leo Oppenheimer, in the department of Near Eastern Studies at the University of Chicago, estimates that about ninety percent of the ancient cuneiform writings from Sumer, Assyria, and Babylon have to do with divination—the attempt to understand the mind of the gods when making important choices (*Ancient Mesopotamia,* University of Chicago, 1964).

People in the ancient world used all kinds of ways to determine the mind of the gods. Some of them studied livers, thinking that the center of thought was in the stomach, not the head. During their divination ritual the priests killed an animal. While the animal was still warm they ripped it open, cut out the liver, and by the motion of the animal's organ— the quiver of the liver—discovered the mind of the gods. In fact, a library in the ancient city of Assurbanipal, Assyria, contained many of the tablets that dealt with the study of livers as an aid in divination.

Today we no longer believe in the mystical powers of the stomach, even though it sometimes seems as if we're thinking with our stomachs rather than our heads! But the legacy of this ancient belief remains in our language, particularly when someone says they made a gut decision or "just felt it in their gut."

Other people in the ancient world consulted the stars. Astrology, as we know it today, came into existence around the fifth or sixth century B.C. in Persia. Astrologers divided the heavens into houses, and depending on the date of your birth and the time of day you were born, you had a place in a particular house. As the stars moved your stars were sometimes in a position to bring you luck. These provided the most fortuitous seasons for kings to sign treaties, for armies to go into battle, and for businessmen to enter into special contracts.

Others in ancient Greece and Rome consulted oracles. Oracles were priests or priestesses who supposedly had divine enablement to know the mind of the gods and to predict the future. What they actually possessed was a special skill to give a general answer that sounded specific. For example, if a military commander went to the oracle to get counsel as to whether or not to go to battle, the oracle might say something like this: "Go, and a great army will be defeated." The commander would take this as a positive statement that he should go off to battle. If he won, he was sure that the oracle had given him sound advice. On the other hand, if he lost the battle and came back looking for that oracle, the oracle might shrug and say, "Well, I said that if you went to battle, a great army would be defeated. Yours is a great army, and as you can see, your army was defeated."

We're not sure of the life expectancy for individual oracles when their vague predictions resulted in kings losing wars, but the practice of consulting oracles lasted a few hundred years until the generals, kings, and businessmen realized that something was wrong.

The Silence of the Bible

When we understand the ancient world's preoccupation with various practices of divination, it's surprising to note that nowhere in the Old Testament, the teachings of Jesus, or the New Testament epistles do we see any description of a step-by-step process by which we can determine God's will.

As we have seen, this silence isn't because divination wasn't a major preoccupation of the times. Quite the contrary, divination was a consuming passion of the pagans. Perhaps that's part of the reason that God, in His Word, expressly forbids divination and similar practices. Read what God tells His people:

> "Let no one be found among you who sacrifices his son or daughter in the fire, who practices divination or sorcery, interprets omens, engages in witchcraft, or casts spells, or who is a medium or spiritist or who consults the dead. Anyone who does these things is detestable to the LORD, and because of these detestable practices, the LORD your God will drive out those nations before you." (Deuteronomy 18:10–12)

Divining Christians

Certainly, as twentieth-century Christians, we wouldn't even consider examining a liver to determine God's will. But, unfortunately, many modern followers of Christ do seek guidance in ways dangerously close to divination.

I have a friend who tells me that when he wants to find the mind of God, he sits down in an easy chair, clears his mind of every thought, and asks God to direct him. This friend believes that the first thought to come into his mind is divinely prompted. Now, I have no quarrel with somebody sitting in a chair to think as he's making a decision. But when we lift our inner impressions to the level of divine revelation, we are flirting with divination.

Other people play "biblical roulette" to seek God's direction in their decision-making. They let their fingers walk through the sacred pages, seeking some land of guidance as they scan the surface of God's Word. If a verse pops out at them while they're scanning, they believe that's what God is trying to say to them. Other people play "biblical roulette" by letting the Bible flop open at a particular passage or verse and accept that as the voice of God.

There's a story that has lasted a long time not only because of its humor but also because of its insight. It's about a man attempting to discover the mind of God by taking his chances with the Bible. He simply shut his eyes, opened up his Bible, and put his finger on a passage. Opening his eyes, he read this passage from Matthew 27: "Then he went away and hanged himself." Somehow, the fellow didn't think that gave him any direction for his problem, so he closed his eyes again and opened his Bible to another passage. He looked and read Jesus' statement in Luke 10: "Go and do likewise." That wasn't quite what he was looking for either, so he tried one more time. He shut his eyes, opened his Bible, and read the statement in John 2:5, "Do whatever he tells you."

This ridiculous example makes a point. Many people have treated the Bible as a book of magic and thereby delved into divination. In doing this they have made some disastrous decisions and, even worse, they have used the Bible in a way that is detestable to God.

Another method well-meaning Christians have employed for finding God's will is the use of "promise boxes." You've seen these promise boxes; they're sold in many religious bookstores. The boxes contain cards listing a thousand verses, many of which are taken completely out of their context. For many sincere Christians, these promise boxes have sometimes served as instruments of divination.

A well-known Christian leader faced the impending death of his wife who was in a hospital intensive care unit. One morning as he was eating breakfast before going to the hospital, he noticed the promise box on the kitchen table. He reached in and pulled out a card. It said, "I am the resurrection and the life. He who believes in me will live" (John 11:25). Struck by the promise of the verse, he put it back in and reached in and pulled out a second card. It said, "I shall not die, but live, and declare the works of the LORD" (Psalm 118:17, NKJV).

The man was convinced that God had spoken to him. With the elation of his newfound inspiration, he left for the hospital filled with joy, convinced that God was going to raise up his wife and bring back her health again. He testified to his wife's nurses that God was going to perform a miracle. The next morning, his wife died. Not only was this good man crushed, but the name of God was blasphemed in that hospital. People observing this bizarre chain of events could choose their conclusion—either the man was a religious fanatic or God had gone back on His promise.

Filling in the Blanks

When we grow unhappy with the results of our promise boxes and displeased with the lack of a surefire biblical plan for knowing God's specific will, we often adopt pet theories to help us find God's great plan. People constantly ask how they can know God's will, and apparently some have decided there must be an easy answer.

In my youth, advice for confronting the important decision, "Whom should I marry?" came freely in short sessions at summer camp. Today we attend expensive single's conferences complete with specialized sessions on dating and hefty notebooks. But the answer to the "whom" question often remains, "God chooses best for those who leave the choice with Him."

That sounded reasonable when I was asking the question. But I still struggled with how I would know the woman God had chosen for me. Would she wear her hair in a special way, or carry an extremely large Scofield Bible? Or would I see a sign—say a lightening bolt with our initials nicely etched in a heart-shaped pattern?

Unfortunately, it was at the point of asking for more specifics that answers became more vague.

When I was in seminary, I had a professor who used to say, "God always speaks loud enough for the willing heart to hear." That, too, seemed to be eminently good counsel. My heart was *willing,* or at least it was willing to be made willing. But what my professor didn't tell us was precisely how the willing heart hears. Would I have a hunch that felt particularly inspired or perhaps a warm feeling in my willing heart?

Later, I encountered the bull's-eye theory of the will of God. Those who espoused this view seemed to think that there was a range of possible choices that were acceptable to God, but that our main goal should be to hit God's bull's-eye. These people would say, "Look, it's not enough to be in God's will; what you want is to be in the center of God's will." Usually the people in the center of God's will were professional Christians—presidents of seminaries, pastors, and especially missionaries. Then there were people in the next concentric ring right outside the bull's-eye—the staff of a seminary and Christian businesspeople supporting pastors and missionaries. Then there were the folks who were one ring farther out. They went to church but weren't quite as involved in God's work as the others. Finally, we had those who missed that target completely. These poor souls had missed God's will and didn't have a chance of returning to that bull's-eye. Amazingly, this bull's-eye theology was taught as though the authority of the Scripture was behind it.

But the question, *How do I know God's will?* seemed legitimate and since thoughtful Christians asked it, many Christian leaders felt they had to provide an answer.

The Three Wills of God

One reason for the confusion is that we aren't always clear about what we mean when we use the term *God's will*. Philosophers are right when they demand that we define our terms. Once we define what we're talking about, the term *God's will* can really mean different things.

God's Sovereign Will

Sometimes the Bible speaks about God's sovereign will. This is God's purpose from eternity past to eternity future whereby He determines all that shall take place. That's what

Paul has in mind when he wrote, "In him we were also chosen, having been predestined according to the plan of him who works out everything in conformity with the purpose of his will" (Ephesians 1:11). In essence, Paul was saying that history is God's story and that He writes the story line.

Theologians sometimes call this God's hidden will or His secret will because He doesn't necessarily reveal it to His people. Occasionally we catch a glimpse of it. For example, the Jews knew from Old Testament times that the Messiah would be born in Bethlehem of Judea. But we see it primarily in retrospect. We read history books to review what has taken place, and even then can't be sure God's sovereign will was properly interpreted.

God has a sovereign will, and He chooses to reveal parts of it to us. But we are treading presumptuously on holy ground when we too readily identify our will—or the actions of our church, organization, or movement—with His will. Much of God's sovereign will is hidden from us, shrouded in mystery and majesty.

God's Moral Will

The second level of the will of God is God's moral will. We have much of this—or at least what God wanted us to know—revealed to us in the Bible. The Scriptures tell us what God wants us to believe and how God wants us to behave. This is the moral will of God, and it is clear.

God's Individual Will

There is yet a third level of God's will in which many people believe: God's individual will. This is what we are usually concerned about when we ask, "How can I know God's will?"

When it comes to God's individual will, we seem to believe that God has our lives mapped out on a blackboard in heaven, and that we must see it to make the choices God desires for us.

In fact, Scripture tells us that God uses even atheists and unbelievers, those who surely aren't seeking it, to bring about God's will. Peter, speaking about Christ's death in Jerusalem on the Day of Pentecost, said to the people in his hearing, "This man was handed over to you by God's set purpose and foreknowledge; and you, with the help of wicked men, put him to death by nailing him to the cross" (Acts 2:23). Christ's violent death on the cross had been planned in eternity past, and when those Roman soldiers carried out the crucifixion it was not because they sensed they were doing God's will.

God works out His sovereign will through all men and women. He has revealed to us His moral will. But He doesn't necessarily reveal His specific, individual will to us. It's possible that He does this at special times for some Christians, but we have no solid biblical testimony on that point. Unfortunately, this hasn't stopped many Christians from putting God's individual will on the same biblical footing as God's sovereign and moral will.

Misusing Our Main Tool

In fact, in our attempt to discern God's will, we frequently misuse the Bible. While Scripture is our main tool for finding God's will, a number of books on the subject mistranslate, misapply, or ignore the context of Bible verses they use to support their theories. Let's look at a few of the passages commonly misused.

One passage frequently misapplied is Proverbs 3:5–6. The King James Version says, "Trust in the LORD with all thine heart, and lean not unto thine own understanding. In all thy ways acknowledge him, and he shall direct thy paths." The New International Version ends verse 6 with "and he will make your paths straight." Writers often interpret these verses to mean that we will get specific direction every day in the choices we make. That's not what the wise man is saying. Verse 6 promises only that God will make our paths smooth or straight.

Proverbs 11:5 uses the same phrase again: "The righteousness of the blameless makes a straight way for them, but the wicked are brought down by their own wickedness." In other words, the wicked fall flat on their faces, but the path of those who are righteous resembles a straight highway.

Look also at Proverbs 4:18–19: "The path of the righteous is like the first gleam of dawn, shining ever brighter till the full light of day. But the way of the wicked is like deep darkness; they do not know what makes them stumble." Very simply, this says that if you walk in the wisdom of God, you won't trip and fall; but the wicked follow a dark and troubled way. The wicked don't even know what makes them stumble; they can't see all the traps along the way.

In the context of the book of Proverbs the instrument for knowing God is His Word (see Proverbs 2).

Peace as Proof

One popular teaching on God's will declares that a sense, or feeling, of peace confirms that we are following God's will for our lives. A verse often misused in such discussions is Colossians 3:15: "Let the peace of Christ rule in your hearts,

since as m   body you were called to peace." This
passage i   that peace proves we are in God's will.

So   his text explain that a possible transla-
tion of the word   e is our word *umpire.* You know you are
in God's will, they argue, because you enjoy a feeling of peace
as long as you remain within God's boundaries. Once you step
over these divine boundaries, the heavenly umpire's whistle
blows and you experience turmoil in your life. According to
this interpretation, you must literally let the peace of Christ
rule in your heart determining each specific decision.

This sounds plausible, but the passage isn't talking
about decision-making, and Paul wasn't referring to inner
peace. In the previous verses he said, "Bear with each other
and forgive whatever grievances you may have against one
another. Forgive as the Lord forgave you. And over all these
virtues put on love, which binds them all together in perfect
unity. Let the peace of Christ rule in your hearts since as
members of one body you were called to peace. And be thank-
ful" (Colossians 3:13–15).

Paul was not offering guidelines for making decisions.
He was emphasizing that God's will is that we live in harmony with one another. That's it. The passage has nothing to do
with the process of making major life decisions.

If we think about it, peace cannot be the proof that we're
in God's will. If ever anyone was in God's will, it was our Lord
Jesus Christ. But the Bible tells us that just before His crucifixion, Jesus sweat great drops of blood. With strong cries and
tears He asked that, if possible, this cup be taken from Him
(Luke 22:41–44). At that moment Jesus fulfilled the will of
His Father in heaven, but if these are the marks of a man at
peace, it's certainly a strange kind of peace.

Look at a contrasting example. If ever anyone was out of God's will, it was Jonah. God commanded Jonah to go to Nineveh, which was to the north and to the east. But Jonah, the reluctant prophet, immediately headed to the south and to the west, and boarded a ship sailing out into the Mediterranean. After the boat put out to sea, a tremendous storm arose, and the pagan sailors were terrified.

But Jonah didn't worry—he was asleep in the lower deck of the boat. He had peace, perfect peace, in the midst of the storm. Yet the prophet was completely out of the will of God.

These accounts of Jesus and Jonah demonstrate that inner peace cannot signal whether or not we are in God's will. Scripture simply does not uphold such a theory.

The Long Shadow of the Early Church

One of the more complicated questions that arises in a discussion of decision-making is "Do you believe the early church had divine guidance?" Undoubtedly the early church had very clear guidance. Three passages from the book of Acts make that evident.

First, let's look at Philip's encounter with the Ethiopian eunuch. "Now an angel of the Lord said to Philip, 'Go south to the road—the desert road—that goes down from Jerusalem to Gaza' " (Acts 8:26). As Philip was on his way he met an Ethiopian eunuch, an important official in charge of the entire treasury of Candace, queen of the Ethiopians. The Ethiopian man had gone to Jerusalem to worship, and on the way home he was sitting in his chariot reading the book of Isaiah. "The Spirit told Philip, 'Go to that chariot and stay near it' " (8:29). And Philip went.

God's guidance was more than a hunch; it was direct, divine intervention in Philip's life. Philip didn't have a sudden compelling sense that his Samaritan ministry was ending, or a deep feeling that God wanted him to start a new ministry down in Gaza to charioteers on their way to Egypt. Scripture is clear that the word came from an angel of the Lord who told Philip to go to that place, and when he got there, the Spirit said, "Join thyself to this chariot" (KJV). This is not an impression or a feeling, but direct, specific verbal guidance from God.

We find a second example of God's guidance in the early church in Acts 10.

> At Caesarea there was a man named Cornelius, a centurion in what was known as the Italian Regiment. He and all his family were devout and God-fearing; he gave generously to those in need and prayed to God regularly. One day at about three in the afternoon he had a vision. He distinctly saw an angel of God, who came to him and said, "Cornelius!"
>
> Cornelius stared at him in fear. "What is it, Lord?" he asked.
>
> The angel answered, "Your prayers and gifts to the poor have come up as a memorial offering before God. Now send men to Joppa to bring back a man named Simon who is called Peter. He is staying with Simon the tanner, whose house is by the sea." (Acts 10:1–6)

The name *Joppa* did not flash in and out of Cornelius' mind, nor did he suddenly decide he ought to go there because he had an inner compulsion. Instead, an angel came to him and commanded, "Go down to Joppa." The angel revealed to Cornelius a specific place and a specific location where he would find a specific man to bring back. Cornelius wasn't dreaming or hallucinating. Like Philip, he received direct, specific verbal guidance from an angelic messenger of God.

A third example of direct divine guidance is recorded in Acts 16, which describes a vision Paul received as he was traveling in Asia Minor. In this divine vision, Paul saw a man from Macedonia asking him to "come over and help" the Macedonians. As a result of that vision, Paul began to evangelize these people.

One striking similarity in these three instances of divine guidance is that they pushed the early believers to share the gospel with people they may not have thought of reaching. Luke's purpose in recording these events was not to identify a means for receiving direct guidance from God when we have to decide whether to marry a particular person, take a different job, or move to a new location. If we're going to wait for that kind of direction, we may wait a very long time.

Fleecing Ourselves

Perhaps the most misused Bible passage is the account of Gideon's fleece. The story begins with the Lord's appearance to Gideon, commissioning him to lead Israel's rebellion against the conquering Midianites. Gideon was overwhelmed. "If you will save Israel by my hand as you have promised— look, I will place a wool fleece on the threshing floor. If there is dew only on the fleece and all the ground is dry, then I will know that you will save Israel by my hand, as you said" (Judges 6:36—37). And sure enough, that's what happened. Gideon arose early the next day, squeezed the fleece, and wrung out the dew—a bowlful of water.

Not wanting to rush to any uncertain conclusions, Gideon decided a second test was in order! " 'Do not be angry with me. Let me make just one more request. Allow me one more test with the fleece. This time make the fleece dry and the ground covered with dew.' That night God did so. Only the fleece was dry; all the ground was covered with dew" (Judges 6:39–40).

The experiences Gideon had with the fleece were truly amazing. For the fleece to be soaking wet while the ground was dry was nothing short of miraculous. And for the fleece to be dry when the ground was wet was equally astounding. Based on that incident in the Old Testament, many Christians try to determine God's will by "putting out a fleece." What they do usually has little to do with Gideon's test.

The first winter I was at Denver Seminary, one of the students was chatting with me about the Christmas break. She told me she was thinking of going skiing, but she was seeking the mind of God as to whether or not she ought to go. I asked her how she expected to determine God's will on the matter. Very matter-of-factly she said, "Well, I put out a fleece. If my daddy sends me some money, then I'll know that skiing is something God wants me to do."

I thought for a moment, and asked her, "Does your father send you money very often?" "Oh, yes," she said, "about three or four times a year. I haven't asked him for any money lately, and I figure if he sends me money I'll know God wants me to go skiing."

I appreciated her faith and her willingness to submit even the mundane decisions of her life to the guidance of God. But I thought she was undervaluing Gideon's experiences with the fleece.

"Look," I asked her, "if you're really going to put out a fleece, why not a good one? After all, if you go skiing and you're not in God's will, you might break your neck. Why don't you pray that the president will send you a letter, and in that letter there will be a check that will give you enough to go skiing? And if you're really going to follow Gideon's example to the limit, pray that you get a second letter and a check from Britain's prime minister the next day. When you get both checks, back-to-back, you can be assured that God wants you to go skiing. That's the type of miraculous sign that Gideon wanted from God. His odds weren't 70–30; he was asking for two miracles, and he got them both!"

If we carelessly apply Gideon's case to our decisions, we are only fleecing ourselves—and we may be keeping ourselves from following God's will when He has given it to us in a much clearer form.

A Sure Source of God's Guidance

As you've been reading this chapter you may have wondered whether I believe God guides us at all. You might think, "If he believes God guides us, I haven't seen any evidence of it yet!"

Let me make this clear. Christians have guidance. It's unambiguous and direct. It's from God, it's for us, and it's found in His Word.

Paul wrote in 2 Timothy 3:16 that all Scripture is "God-breathed," or inspired by God. This means that the Bible is to God what breath is to a man or a woman—it comes out of His innermost being. Then Paul said that this God-breathed volume is profitable for four things. It's profitable for teaching us what we ought to believe. It's profitable for rebuke; it tells us when we've gone wrong. It's profitable for correction; it gets us back on the path again. And it's profitable for instruction in right living.

But all of this is designed to do one thing—to thoroughly equip the man or woman of God to do every good work.

This is important. This God-breathed book is not only inspired, but when we understand and apply it correctly, it is all-sufficient, giving us all we need for all life's decisions so that we might be all that God wants us to be. For us to live according to the Scriptures is to live in the will of God.

The Crowd Waits Anxiously

It's the day Jesus is to come to Los Angeles for a press conference. (Such an event may not fit into everybody's eschatology, but please bear with me.) At the meeting, we've been promised Jesus will tell us how we can know the will of God.

A large coalition of religious leaders has rented the Coliseum in Los Angeles to hold the crowd that's anticipated to come and hear Jesus speak. The story is scheduled to lead all three U.S. network news broadcasts; satellites will beam the story around the world. Stories and photos from the Coliseum will get page-one treatment in every paper in the country.

Inside the mammoth Coliseum, packed to the rafters with anxious seekers, at last Jesus comes to the podium.

To the amazement of all, Jesus steps up to the microphone but doesn't say a word. He simply holds up a book, the Bible, and says, "I have given you my Word. All that you need to know for faith and practice is in this book. It is enough not only for your eternal salvation, but for your guidance through life. Read it. Follow it. Then you will know God's will."

I don't know if you would be disappointed if you were in that crowd—or how the press would portray such a daring presentation—but it's the truth. God has spoken, and His Word guides us.

2

Decision-Making and the Word of God

All Scripture is God-breathed and is useful for teaching, rebuking, correcting and training in righteousness, so that the man of God may be thoroughly equipped for every good work.

(2 Timothy 3:16–17)

The history of our world resembles a high-stress poker game. At least that's the way American historian Samuel Eliot Morison saw it.

Morison pictured the nations of the world sitting around a table, each of them being dealt several hands of cards. Some of the nations had consistently good hands; some, consistently poor hands; most, a mixture.

As time passed, some of the nations with good hands played them poorly and came away losers. A few with bad hands played shrewdly and came away winners. Some at the table didn't play at all; they simply sat and let the game go on around them.

Morison observed that things are the same for individuals as nations. How we fare in life isn't merely a matter of the cards we are dealt, but how we play the game.

Taking a Peek Into the Future

One thing all card players wish they could do is to get a look at the cards as they are dealt. Some unscrupulous gamblers do just that by marking the deck. Since they know what cards are coming, they are able to anticipate the future; they know when to raise the bid and when to drop out of the game.

Millions of people trying to get ahead in the game of life are also very interested in getting a look at the cards in the deck. Throughout history people have thought, "If only we could anticipate the future, if only we could know the cards coming into play, then we would feel much less vulnerable when making decisions in life."

Certainly those of us who are Christians understand the anxiety that drives people to such extremes—especially in the choices that seem most significant in our lives.

When we face life's tough decisions—where we make choices over what vocation to enter, what school to attend, what job to take, what ministry to give ourselves to—we often feel very vulnerable, and the awesomeness of the choice comes in upon us and increases our fear of doing the wrong thing.

Christians, like their pagan neighbors, have wanted to get a glimpse of the deck—or at least to get an inside track in the mind of the dealer—and thus increase their chances for a better payoff when the game is over.

The Christian Crystal Ball

Through the ages, Christians have done all kinds of things to get a glimpse of the mind of God. Some of them have turned the Bible into a book of magic. They have let the Scriptures flop open on their desk and allowed their eye to drift down the page. And when a line or verse leaps up at them—in or out of context, it doesn't matter—they take that to be the mind of God.

Others, instead of gazing at the stars, gaze at circumstances. They try to read what is happening in their lives—the same way a palmist reads lines on a hand—and from that determine what God is doing.

Still others have gone with a carefully developed system of intuition and hunches. They often lift their inner impressions to the level of divine revelation and claim that God spoke to them. Perhaps not audibly, they say, but He spoke. They have gotten some glimpse into God's mind and now they know what they are supposed to do—at least for the next hand.

Such practices are so common—and the anxiety that leads to them is so understandable—that we are shocked when we turn to the Bible and discover that asking the question: "How do we know the will of God for life's tough decisions?" isn't a biblical question!

God does not encourage us to ask the question and even more significantly, God gives us no answer. The Bible's silence almost shouts at us.

God's Word Is Sufficient

But God did give us the Bible, which itself is sufficient to guide us. The problem is that so many of our important decisions aren't addressed in the Bible. No chapter is devoted to whether we should attend one college instead of another. No passage tells us what job to take or which person to marry.

For some, talk of the Bible's sufficiency seems to leave us back in the dusty, ancient past of two thousand years ago. *How can that give us any help for today?* we wonder. But that reaction indicates we're not taking the Bible very seriously. One of the things that the Bible teaches us, for example, is that God is working out His will. The God whom we worship is sovereign in the affairs of men and nations, and He works out all things according to His purposes. God is at work in our lives, and He is at work in the world.

The difficulty with God's sovereign will is that we do not always see Him at work. It is hidden, removed from our observation. But we know it's there—particularly after an event happens and we think we can see His purposes more clearly.

For example, when Jesus came to earth, He did not come unannounced. Prophets in the ancient days anticipated His coming and predicted that He would be born in Bethlehem of Judea. They predicted He would be born of a virgin. What is more, they told us in general terms the kind of death He would die, and in very specific terms that He would be placed in the tomb of a wealthy man. The psalmist announced beforehand that He would rise from the dead.

Today, we confidently look forward to Christ's second coming. And in the books of Daniel and Revelation, we are given rather specific counsel as to what will take place before He comes. Though the picture is not crystal clear to us, there are signs to watch for.

Mysteries of God's Will and Our Wills

In this life, our wills and God's will are strangely partnered. Peter spoke to this mystery when he preached to the crowd cramming the streets of Jerusalem at Pentecost:

> "This man was handed over to you by God's set purpose and foreknowledge; and you, with the help of wicked men, put him to death by nailing him to the cross. But God raised him from the dead." (Acts 2:23—24)

The implication of this brief passage is profound. Peter acknowledged that when the people of Jerusalem crucified Jesus, they made their own choices. The Roman soldiers *chose* to follow orders and drive spikes into His hands. Pilate *chose* to make ambition his guide and delivered Jesus to be crucified. The religious leaders *chose* to egg the people on to ask that Barabbas be set free and Jesus crucified. There were all kinds of choices made that day. And all these independently made choices were subsumed into God's infinite will and purpose.

If we had been there on what we now call Good Friday, we would never have called it good. We would have called it Bleak Friday, for it was the day that the best man ever known was nailed to a Roman execution rack. The awful hour of His crucifixion seemed certain proof that wrong was on the throne and right was on the scaffold.

But Peter said that bleak Friday was merely a prelude to glorious Sunday when Christ rose from the dead. That is the sovereign working of God. The people of Jerusalem were responsible for their choices, but in their choices—through that awful agony of crucifixion—God brought His best.

The View from Bleak Friday

Someone has said that life is what happens to you after you've made your decisions. There are times when we make our decisions as best we can, and suddenly life crumbles in on us. The unanticipated becomes the dominant force in our lives. It seems that wrong has triumphed and right has been trampled underfoot. It may seem that men and women in their rebellion against God have won the revolution. But that's Friday; in God's sovereign will Sunday's coming!

God is involved in history. History ultimately is God's story. John Calvin captured this truth in his theology. He recognized that God's eye isn't merely *over* history, but God's hand is *on* history.

We need to remember that when we talk about making decisions, God is not at the mercy of our choices. God is not limited to what we decide to do. But in God's sovereignty, He can work *in* our choices, *through* our choices, and *in spite of* our choices, to accomplish His will.

We may not choose to help, we may not be able to see; but God is at work in the affairs of people and nations to bring about His sovereign will.

God's Moral Will

Not only do theologians talk about God's sovereign will, but also God's moral will. The Scriptures tell us God's moral will for the living of our lives. We are given specific commands as well as general objectives.

For example, one thing we know is that the moral will of God for us as His children is that we are to live for His glory. As Peter wrote:

> Above all, love each other deeply, because love covers over a multitude of sins. Offer hospitality to one another without grumbling. Each one should use whatever gift he has received to serve others, faithfully administering God's grace in its various forms. If anyone speaks, he should do it as one speaking the very words of God. If anyone serves, he should do it with the strength God provides, so that in all things God may be praised through Jesus Christ. To him be the glory and the power for ever and ever. Amen. (1 Peter 4:8–11)

Knowing that this is the goal of our lives helps us in what may seem to be ordinary decisions. In *Alice in Wonderland,* Alice comes to a crossroads and doesn't know which road to take. The Cheshire cat asks, "Well, where are you going?" "I don't know," Alice replies. "Well, if you don't know where you're going," the cat wisely answers, "any road will do very nicely."

If our lives are not repeatedly dedicated to the glory of God, then any choice we make is as good—or as bad—as the next.

Ultimate and Intermediate Goals

The Bible is clear that glorifying God is our ultimate goal. But it doesn't leave us with vague generalities—in achieving that goal, we are given intermediate goals. We are instructed to tell others about Christ, to serve them, to teach them. All of these actions bring glory to God.

God wants the knowledge of His moral will to habitually inform our minds and hearts. In many of life's decisions, that knowledge determines our choices.

God's moral will also limits the means available for reaching the goal. The Bible says that we are to strive within God's boundaries. Paul warned Timothy that an athlete is not crowned unless he strives lawfully. We can't step out of bounds. We can't take a shortcut through the stands at a football game simply because we think that's the way to score a touchdown.

Likewise, no illegal shortcuts ever glorify God. We cannot lie. We cannot stand in a meeting and tell people something God has done for us if He has not done it. We may want God to look good, but we are not allowed to disobey Him to accomplish it.

Wisdom is important, too. Writing to the Ephesians, Paul said that we must be wise to know what the will of God is. Specifically, he explained how a husband is to relate to his wife, a wife to her husband, a father to his children, a child to his parents, as well as how we are to relate to those for whom we work and those who work with and for us.

We are to proceed lawfully; we are to proceed wisely. In these and many other passages we are told the means by which we achieve the goal of bringing glory to God.

The Importance of Motives

God is also very concerned about our motives. The Scriptures teach that what we are is far more important to God than *where* we are; *why* we do something more than *what* we do. Motives can be everything.

We all know it is good to contribute to the church, but if—like the Pharisees—we drop our huge wad of bills into the plate so that people think we're big-time givers, we are out of God's moral will.

Likewise, it's marvelous to be a person of prayer, but if we pray so that folks will be impressed with our tone of voice and choice of words, we've missed God's will. Motive is just as important as action.

God's Guidance for Decision-Making

As we have clearly seen, the Bible gives us a great deal of instruction on God's will. God—through His inspired Word—gives us the comfort of knowing we live in His sovereignty and He gives us the specific direction of His moral will. He spells out our ultimate goal and more immediate goals.

God's direction is clear and unambiguous. We are to act in love and kindness. We are not to be self-serving. We are to have integrity. We are to be faithful and generous. And we are to act out of proper motives.

If we apply the characteristics of God's sovereign and moral will to every decision we make, we will be well on the road to glorifying Him and living a fuller, happier life.

3

The Freedom to Decide

If some unbeliever invites you to a meal and you want to go, eat whatever is put before you without raising questions of conscience.

(1 Corinthians 10:27)

God gives us plenty of help in understanding His sovereign and moral will, and He shows us how our knowledge of His will should guide our decision-making. But what about God's will in our personal situations, what we called His individual will? Here we need to acknowledge a related—and tremendously important—truth about making godly decisions.

That truth is this: When it comes to the decisions that are within God's moral will, we have a great deal of freedom. It's not absolute freedom; it's freedom bound by our concern for others.

Pagan Meat and Spiked Fruit Cake

God doesn't have all of our life's decisions intricately described in some kind of movie script. He does not spell out all the minute details of our lives. Instead, He leaves many choices to us.

We see this truth throughout the Bible. In 1 Corinthians, Paul acknowledged our freedom to make decisions in controversial situations. As Paul wrote, "If some unbeliever invites you to a meal and you want to go, eat whatever is put before you without raising questions of conscience" (1 Corinthians 10:27).

From our perspective, Paul's statement doesn't seem too radical. Many Christians routinely pick up a quick meal with non-Christian coworkers or associates. But in Paul's day—and for the Christians in Corinth—this passage was a shocking proclamation of Christian freedom.

In ancient cities like Corinth, the best meat markets were located at the pagan temple. When worshipers brought their sacrifices to an idol, only a small part of the animal was actually put on the altar. Another part was given as an honorarium to the priest. A third part was given back to the worshipers to take home.

There was no refrigeration in those days (that came about nineteen hundred years later). The priests were often stuck with a lot of meat at the end of the day and since they couldn't store it, they had to sell it. As a result, the temples in most cities housed meat markets; the priests' meat was sold and the money was returned to the temple treasury.

The worshiper too had to use up his meat quickly, and this often meant having a feast. If a worshiper had a house big enough for all his friends, the party would be held at his home. If not, there were rooms close to the temple where they could all enjoy a banquet together.

This meant that the prime rib served in a pagan dinner had been offered in an idol's temple that morning. In Corinth, the meat would have been offered to the goddess Aphrodite. She was the goddess of sexual love and the various practices involved in her worship were totally abhorrent to Christians.

Because of this, an invitation to a banquet presented a Christian with all kinds of problems—theological, emotional, psychological, and spiritual. *What are they going to do at this feast?* a Christian might wonder after receiving his invitation—*Are they going to serve idols' meat?*

When writing to the Corinthian Christians about this sticky problem, Paul didn't tell them to seek the face of God. He didn't say, "This issue is between you and God. Let Him show you whether you ought to go or not." Instead Paul said,

"Look, if you want to go, go and eat. The decision is up to you. There is nothing morally negative or positive about attending a dinner party."

Of course, if a Christian attended a feast, he or she might encounter some unsettling social situations. Paul covered one of these delicate issues: "Eat whatever is put before you without raising questions of conscience. But if anyone says to you, 'This has been offered in sacrifice,' then do not eat it, both for the sake of the man who told you and for conscience' sake" (1 Corinthians 10:27–28).

Putting it in our language, Paul might say, "Go, have a good time; and don't make a big deal about asking where they got the meat. Don't climb a flagpole to make an issue when you can stay on the ground and keep the peace."

Today, Paul might say, "If you abstain from alcohol, don't spend your entire evening at the neighborhood Christmas party trying to figure out if the fruitcake contains rum. Just assume that it's rum flavoring and eat it. If, however, the brother sitting next to you nudges you and says, 'I know you don't drink, and that's why I need to tell you that this fruitcake is full of rum,' then don't eat any!"

Neither our Christmas party nor the Corinthians' feast is any place to have a theological discussion with a brother. Why? Because, as Paul said in verse 24, "Nobody should seek his own good, but the good of others."

In other words, if what I want to do conflicts with what is best for someone else, then I will go with the other person's best. I still have my freedom. If I'm the only Christian at the feast and nobody brings it up, I can eat the meat.

But if the host says, "This has come from Aphrodite and she always gives us the best to eat; let us enjoy ourselves in her honor," I had better decide to skip the meat and only eat the vegetables. I've got to make the choice to eat or not to eat on the basis of godly principles.

Free to Choose a Mate

If there's one decision for which a thoughtful Christian wants some guidance, it's the question, "Whom should I marry?" After all, we link ourselves to a mate for life. (By the way, that's God's will for Christians.) This is a pretty important decision, so surely God has an ideal mate picked out for each of us. Paul dealt with this issue, too: "A woman is bound to her husband as long as he lives. But if her husband dies, she is free to marry anyone she wishes, but he must belong to the Lord. In my judgment, she is happier if she stays as she is—and I think that I too have the Spirit of God" (1 Corinthians 7:39–40).

The moral will of God when it comes to marriage is that you marry another believer. That's all Paul said to the widow whose husband had died—your fiancé must belong to the Lord. Within that boundary she could marry anyone she chose—as long as that person also chose her, of course!

At the same time, Paul suggested that not marrying is a better option. As he said in verses 32–34, single people have more freedom to serve the Lord, while married people are more concerned with pleasing their mates. But even after making his argument for singleness, Paul added, "I am saying this for your own good, not to restrict you" (v. 35). Paul favored the single life. But again, the choice—whether to marry or not to marry, or whom to marry—is up to the individual believer.

If a believer wanted to marry, Paul did not prohibit it. The only boundary the Christian needs to stay within is that the mate must also be a believer. If you marry an unbeliever, you have stepped out of God's moral will. But if you marry a Christian, it is within that framework that you must make the decision of whom to marry. You don't necessarily marry any Christian who comes along, of course. You must weigh the pros and cons, but the choice is up to you.

Freedom and Responsibility

God cares about the decisions we make, and certainly each decision confronts us with choices, some of which are ultimately better than others. But the message of this chapter is that if we make our decisions within the boundaries of God's sovereign and moral will, we have a great deal of freedom.

The question we should ask is no longer, "What is God's will?" Instead, the question is, "How do I make good decisions?" If we change the question, we change the direction of the answer.

To ask the question, "How do I know God's will?" makes us passive. But to ask the question, "How do I make good decisions?" makes us active. It shifts the responsibility of decision-making from God to us. God has given us the freedom to make good decisions, and we're responsible for them. It's in making decisions according to God's moral will that we become the kind of people God wants us to be.

When our children were small, my wife and I gave them a great deal of guidance. We stood at the sidewalk and we held them by the hand and said, "You hold on tight to my hand. We'll go across this street together." And, for the most part, it worked—at least they didn't get killed.

Then, when they got a bit older, we changed our approach. We would accompany them to the street corner, where we would stop and say, "Now, when the light turns red and the cars stop, you can cross." Fearfully at first, we let them go alone.

It's been a long time since I stood at the corner with my son or daughter, hand-in-hand, to help them cross the street. In fact, it would be laughable to do something like that with mature adult children. Instead, my children now have a great deal of freedom in crossing the streets, and they exercise that freedom!

In God's sovereignty, according to His moral will, we have the freedom—and the responsibility—to choose. The question, "How do I know God's will?" becomes, "How do I make good decisions?"

In the next section we will examine biblical principles that will help make us better decision-makers.

4

Submitting to God's Sovereign Will

Now listen, you who say, "Today or tomorrow we will go to this or that city, spend a year there, carry on business and make money." Why, you do not even know what will happen tomorrow. What is your life? You are a mist that appears for a little while and then vanishes. Instead, you ought to say, "If it is the Lord's will, we will live and do this or that." As it is, you boast and brag. All such boasting is evil.

(James 4:13–16)

everal years ago I spoke with a woman—a new believer—about a decision she had made to visit some relatives in California. She told me she had not been sure that going to California was in God's will, so one morning she went to her room and prayed for God's direction. While she was on her knees, she glanced up at her digital clock; it read "7:47." She knew that "747" was the name of a jet airplane and was sure that God had told her, through the numbers on the face of the digital clock, to go to California.

I must confess, I was not convinced. I would have been more impressed if the clock had read "7:67" or "DC-10!" Such an occurrence would have been truly amazing—maybe even miraculous. But to turn a rather run-of-the-mill coincidence into a portentous sign of divine guidance is dangerous!

Realizing I was not overly impressed by her "sign," the woman asked me, "Don't you think God can speak to Christians that way?" Of course, God can do anything God wants to do. He can even speak through a jackass—and according to His Word He has done just that (Numbers 22:21–41). But that doesn't mean I go down to the barnyard to get the guidance of God!

Sometimes when we go around trying to know God's will, we do some very silly things. What's worse is that probing for God's will can cause some of us to suffer terrible—and often unnecessary—pain.

My wife and I know a woman who, throughout her life, has made some very bad decisions. She entered into a bad marriage that ended in divorce. And just recently, she decided to enter into a second marriage that seems—to those who know her—just as bad as the first.

One of this woman's friends wanted to help her avoid more pain and spoke to her about this ill-advised second marriage. The woman, full of pain and disappointment, responded, "You know, when I was twenty-one years of age, I gave my life to Jesus Christ. I asked God to show me His will. Now I'm over forty, and He has never shown it to me." This woman made a series of wretched choices that have blighted her life. As she passively waited to see God's will, a pool of resentment, frustration, and anger against God grew within her.

Asking the Right Question

To get a good answer, you have to ask a good question. This simple generality has profound implications for living in a way that glorifies God.

To ask, "How can I know the will of God?" can make us passive in the midst of life's choices. We wait for hunches, impressions, coincidences to come and reveal God's will. We try to study circumstances. And for some people, it can actually lead to disobedience.

Every pastor knows people who say that God has led them to do certain things—things that blatantly contradict the clear teaching of God in Scripture. Such people seem to think that God permits some special things for them that He doesn't allow in the church at large.

We must face the fact: "How do you know the will of God in making life's decisions?" is not a biblical question! The Bible never tells us to ask it. The Bible never gives us direction in answering it. And the pursuit of some personalized version of the "will of God" often leads us toward disobedience. When we find ourselves facing the tough choices in life—those day-in, day-out decisions that make up the very fabric of our existence—we shouldn't seek special messages from God. Instead, we should ask, "How do we develop the skills necessary to make wise and prudent choices?"

The Bible does speak to that question—at length. We should not turn to Scripture in search of a detailed road map. The Bible is not so much a map as it is a compass. It doesn't give us specifics but it does provide direction.

Submitting to God's Sovereign Will

The first principle to follow when we are trying to make choice choices is that we must make our decisions in submission to the sovereign will of God. This is what James meant when he wrote:

> Now listen, you who say, "Today or tomorrow we will go to this or that city, spend a year there, carry on business and make money." Why, you do not even know what will happen tomorrow. What is your life? You are a mist that appears for a little while and then vanishes. Instead, you ought to say, "If it is the Lord's will, we will live and do this or that." As it is, you boast and brag. All such boasting is evil. (James 4:13–16)

We can imagine James opening the door to a first-century boardroom. A group of businessmen are gathered around a table. In front of them is sprawled a map. And one of their number, an expert in marketing, has just given the results of his research. He points to the map and says, "Either one of the two cities is a good prospect. If we go to these cities and take advantage of this opportunity immediately, we can't lose! Within six months we'll be making a profit. Within a year we ought to be able to triple our money!"

To support what he says, this ancient entrepreneur brings out his charts. He reveals the business' goals. He shows the steps to the goal. He has mapped it all out on a detailed timeline. He has repeatedly run the numbers through his abacus. And he has calculated the needed investment and the profit.

And James, entering the room, points to the men gathered around the table and says, "Look, fellas. What you're doing is very dangerous. All these charts, calculations, and predictions display a boastfulness that totally ignores a crucial reality—our plans are not under our control. With all of this planning, you have not planned on God."

A Strong Sense of "If . . ."

To leave God out of our planning is a dangerous thing to do. To paraphrase James' counsel: "Look, you don't even know what will happen tomorrow. You ought to make your plans with a very strong sense of "If," because you don't know what the next day will hold, not to mention the next year."

The writer of Proverbs concurs, "Do not boast about tomorrow, for you do not know what a day may bring forth" (Proverbs 27:1).

The uncertainty of life assails us from all sides. Yesterday's "sure thing" in the market takes a tumble; a failproof business deal comes apart at the seams.

We don't know what tomorrow holds. Certainly we don't know about next year. Our knowledge is limited.

But James went even further. Not only are we unknowing, but we are also impotent. We can't even be sure we'll be here tomorrow! "What is your life?" James asks. "You are a mist that appears for a little while and then vanishes."

Life is that way. It's fragile; it's fleeting. It's like a mist that settles over a valley in the morning. The sun comes up and by ten o'clock, the mist is gone. It's like the steam from a kettle—no sooner does it appear but it disappears. It's like breath on a cold winter's day—now you see it; now you don't.

We may not realize it, but last week's business trip may have brought us within a second or two, within a yard or two, of a fatal crash. Even now a virus may be lurking in our bodies, so small that it cannot be seen without a microscope. But that virus may call us away from our plans, our board meetings, and our comfortable routines, at any time. Life—James tells us—is that way.

We are arrogant, we are proud, and we are boastful if we act as though we know what will happen next in life. We may think that we're the master of our fate, the captain of our soul, or that we will carry out our plans. But we may be in for a terrible surprise.

When I was general director for a Christian medical ministry, one of our physicians told me about a most embarrassing incident that illustrates James' point. One day this doctor conducted a patient's annual physical examination. At the conclusion of the exam, the doctor pronounced the man healthy, giving him a clean bill of health. As the man was leaving the lobby, he fell over dead. Things like that happen in life.

"If It Is the Lord's Will"

When Christians make their decisions, they must do so not only with a strong sense of "If," but also with a strong sense of "If it is the Lord's will." When James says this, he reminds himself and others that God is sovereign. He is the Lord of lords, the King of kings, the God of history, and the Master of life. James calls us to acknowledge that fact when we make our plans. We must remember that everything is subject to God's approval.

But notice, James was not against making plans. When he said, "If the Lord wills, we will do this or that," he was not taking a cheap shot at charts or making an argument against commitments. He wasn't against five-year plans. James warned that our freedom to make plans is not a license to live free from God. To come to that conclusion would be arrogant.

James included a reminder that God opposes the proud and the haughty (James 4:6). What good are our plans if, in the attitude by which we make them, we turn God into our enemy? God promises grace to the humble, not the proud and arrogant. The phrase, "If it is the Lord's will," ought to infect our thinking. It ought to be a standard part of our vocabulary.

When I was growing up, my mother would often write letters. When her letter described some future plans, she would always add the letters "DV" for *deo velenti,* which means "the Lord willing." I don't think she knew much Latin, but she understood the inevitability of life. And certainly it is a wise and prudent thing for Christians to cultivate that in their speech. More followers of Jesus Christ should pepper their conversations with the comment, "If God wills."

An Attitude of Submission

Of course, James did not mean that we should simply add a religious phrase to our vocabulary. He was concerned about a basic attitude that is to pervade our lives, as it pervades the teachings of the Bible.

Look at Paul's attitude of submission to God's will as found in the book of Acts. In one instance, Paul is leaving Ephesus when some of his friends urge him to stay. Paul insisted that he had to leave, but said, "I will come back if it is God's will" (Acts 18:21). It's clear that an attitude acknowledging God's sovereignty was basic to Paul's ministry.

You and I are free to make our decisions, but we are never free from God. We must make our decisions in submission to His sovereign will.

It was Napoleon Bonaparte who, early in his life, said, "God is on the side of the biggest artillery." Years later, when he was exiled on an island, he reversed his opinion, and conceded, "Man proposes, but God disposes." Napoleon learned the attitude of "If it is the Lord's will" the hard way. May we learn it now.

Submission Through Prayer

One of the ways we show our submission to the sovereign will of God is through prayer. There are all kinds of mysteries in prayer, but certainly the purpose of my praying is not for me to tell God how to run His universe. (If that's the case, all of us are in bad shape.) Rather, the purpose of prayer is to bow before the sovereign God and acknowledge His sovereignty in my life and my decisions.

This concept is basic to the Lord's Prayer, where Jesus teaches His disciples to pray. The first three petitions have to do with God—personal needs aren't even addressed until later! Listen to His prayer: "Our Father in heaven, hallowed be your name, your kingdom come, your will be done on earth as it is in heaven" (Matthew 6:9–10).

All too often we go to God to get His confirmation of plans we've made for our own kingdom, glory, and honor. But when we really bow in prayer before God, we acknowledge God's sovereignty. In all our decisions, that attitude must be primary.

Wisdom Through Prayer

When we pray, we can also ask God for wisdom. "If any of you lacks wisdom, he should ask God, who gives generously to all without finding fault, and it will be given to him. But when he asks, he must believe and not doubt" (James 1:5–6). Wisdom in biblical thought is not simply intellectual. It is intellectual *and* moral. As one Bible scholar defined it, wisdom is the endowment of heart and mind needed for the righteous conduct of life.

Wisdom doesn't mean easy answers. The wisdom James described isn't like the one-minute television commercial promising to solve all our dishwashing problems if we buy a certain brand of soap. Wisdom is a moral and a mental state of the heart and mind.

When we pray for wisdom, we open ourselves to God's gifts. God can give us insight into trials. This is the context of His promise in James 1:5. God shows us how He can use any situation to bring us to a richness and ripeness of character that we could not have any other way. That allows us to enter life's most frustrating experiences with a sense of holy optimism. No matter where I am, I can be confident that God can use each situation to make me more like Him.

God can also bring to mind passages from His Word that we have studied or memorized. What is more, He can help us take those passages and apply them to our particular situation.

God has given us tremendous freedom and responsibility in making decisions. When seeking to carry out that responsibility, the place for us to begin is in an attitude of complete submission to the sovereign will of the all-powerful God.

5

Submitting to God's Moral Will

Oh, how I love your law! I meditate on it all day long. Your commands make me wiser than my enemies, for they are ever with me. I have more insight than all my teachers, for I meditate on your statutes. I have more understanding than the elders, for I obey your precepts. I have kept my feet from every evil path so that I might obey your word. I have not departed from your laws, for you yourself have taught me. How sweet are your words to my taste, sweeter than honey to my mouth! I gain understanding from your precepts; therefore I hate every wrong path.

(Psalm 119:97–104)

As we have seen, we must make our decisions in submission to the sovereign will of God. But we must also make our decisions in submission to the moral will of God. Perhaps the best way to understand the difference between God's sovereign will and His moral will is to think about the decision-making processes of an airplane pilot.

A good pilot must have a healthy fear of gravity. This respect isn't in the conscious mind of most pilots, but it forms the foundation of everything they do. When a headstrong pilot comes up against gravity, gravity will win—no matter how strongly the pilot opposes it. A pilot who doesn't respect gravity isn't around to tell us about it! In a sense, this healthy respect of gravity is similar to our living in submission to God's sovereign will. Ultimately, whether or not we choose to accept it, God's will wins out.

But a good pilot must do more than merely respect the law of gravity. A good pilot follows the principles learned from other pilots. He or she must keep the plane straight and level, must avoid stalling the engine. These things help to ensure that the pilot gets the plane to the desired destination safely. The way in which pilots obey these principles of aviation is similar to the way in which all of us must observe the moral will of God, and make our decisions in submission to that moral will.

God's moral will is the abundant counsel of God that is given to us in the Scriptures. These Scriptures deal with our motives, our goals, and the appropriate means for meeting those goals.

As Paul wrote in his letter to Timothy, "All Scripture is God-breathed and is useful for teaching, rebuking, correcting and training in righteousness, so that the man of God may be thoroughly equipped for every good work" (2 Timothy 3:16–17). In other words, all the guidance I need to be all that God wants me to be in all of life's decisions can be found in Scripture.

To make good decisions I need to be mighty in the Word of God. This is not a peripheral issue. I need to know the Scriptures—the New Testament and the Old.

The Bible gives us guidance on everything from A to Z, a fact graphically illustrated by Psalm 119, which features twenty-two sections beginning with the twenty-two letters of the Hebrew alphabet. These sections show us the place of the law of God in a believer's life.

> Oh, how I love your law! I meditate on it all day long. Your commands make me wiser than my enemies, for they are ever with me. I have more insight than all my teachers, for I meditate on your statutes. I have more understanding than the elders, for I obey your precepts. I have kept my feet from every evil path so that I might obey your word. I have not departed from your laws, for you yourself have taught me. How sweet are your words to my taste, sweeter than honey to my mouth! I gain understanding from your precepts; therefore I hate every wrong path. (Psalm 119:97–104)

To make choices while ignoring the Scriptures is to play the fool. Make your decisions in submission to God's moral will.

An Echo or a Revelation?

Submission to God's will is a prerequisite of learning all that God's Word has to tell us. We should not come to the

Bible for confirmation of what we've already decided; instead, we must come to gain God's insight into each decision so that we can make it wisely.

If we don't come in submission to God, the Bible can be a very dangerous book. A person trying to justify a homosexual lifestyle can make the Bible say that homosexuality is acceptable to God if it is a loving relationship between two people of the same sex. The Bible becomes an echo and not a revelation—it tells us what we want to hear.

Most cults and heresies quote the Bible. We can go to hell with a Bible in our hand. We can be destroyed with a Bible verse on our lips. No. We must come to this book determined to submit to its teachings; only then does God make His will known. This point is, of course, illustrated in the Bible.

Ahab and the Truth of God

In the final chapter of the book of 1 Kings we find a compelling example of a man—a follower of God—who went to God for a confirmation of his own beliefs. That man was Ahab, and his story demonstrates how we can turn God's Word into an echo of our own desires.

The story opens as Ahab, King of Israel, was entering into an alliance with Jehoshaphat, king of Judah, apparently through a marriage. But, wanting to formalize the alliance, Ahab urged Jehoshaphat to join him in a battle against the Arameans.

Jehoshaphat came up to Samaria to meet Ahab for a summit conference. After they had made their plans, Jehoshaphat, who apparently was a pious man, reminded Ahab that they needed the Lord's counsel. Obviously, Ahab was prepared for just such a question. He had assembled the national council of the prophets, four hundred strong. He went to his ecumenical council and laid out all his plans for war. The result was unanimous: four hundred to nothing. " 'Go,' they answered, 'for the Lord will give it into the king's hand' " (1 Kings 22:6).

But for some reason Jehoshaphat still wasn't convinced. He was suspicious, like the modern cynic who says, "Well, if you get four hundred preachers all agreeing on something, probably only one of them is thinking and the other three-hundred-ninety-nine are saying 'Amen.' " So Jehoshaphat asked Ahab, "Is there not a prophet of the LORD here whom we can inquire of?" (22:7).

You might think Ahab would be insulted and say to him, "Look, if you can't believe four hundred prophets, what in the world makes you think you can believe four-hundred-one?" But Ahab didn't respond that way. Instead, he said, "There is still one man through whom we can inquire of the LORD, but I hate him because he never prophesies anything good about me, but always bad. He is Micaiah son of Imlah" (22:8).

Jehoshaphat prevailed and Micaiah the prophet was asked to stand before the two kings and announce God's will. Ahab asked Micaiah, "Shall we go to war?" " 'Attack and be victorious,' he answered, 'for the LORD will give it into the king's hand' " (22:15). But Micaiah spoke with heavy sarcasm and Ahab knew it. Ahab demanded that Micaiah tell him the truth. The prophet then told the two kings that he saw Israel scattered on the hills like sheep without a shepherd. In other words, Micaiah promised that if Ahab and Jehoshaphat should go to battle, the results would be disastrous.

Then Micaiah told a story—one of those strange illustrative stories embedded in the Old Testament.

Micaiah said:

> "I saw the LORD sitting on his throne with all the host of heaven standing around him on his right and on his left. And the LORD said, 'Who will entice Ahab into attacking Ramoth Gilead and going to his death there?'
>
> "One suggested this, and another that. Finally, a spirit came forward, stood before the LORD and said, 'I will entice him.'
>
> " 'By what means?' the LORD asked.
>
> " 'I will go out and be a lying spirit in the mouths of all his prophets,' he said." (22:19–22)

This isn't sober history. It's a story. I don't think that God sits on His throne getting advice from spirits as to how to destroy kings. Instead, the force of the story is this: Ahab wanted to believe a lie. Since he wanted to believe a lie, he'd get a lie—even from his prophets. Ahab had already made up his mind. He didn't care about the truth.

As the chapter continues we see how strongly Ahab wanted to believe his prophets' lies. In spite of what Micaiah said, Ahab went to battle. He took the precautionary step of disguising himself, hoping he could ward off death.

Ahab's plan failed. An archer shot an arrow into the air—"at random" Scripture says—and it sunk into Ahab's belly. Isn't it strange how chance and the sovereignty of God meet! The last we read of Ahab, dogs were licking up his rich royal blood by a pool in the capital city of Samaria.

Don't miss the force of that story. If we want to believe a lie, we will get the lie to believe. If we come to the Word of

God determined to do what we please, we can get from the Bible anything we desire.

We must come in submission to the Word, in submission to its teaching, in submission to the moral law of God.

An Attitude of Submission

To make good decisions, we must make them in submission to God's sovereign will and in submission to God's moral will. The attitude of submission must permeate everything we do.

A well-known British scholar was once approached by a woman who said to him, "Professor, it's marvelous to have a man of your intellect who takes his stand on the Word of God." The scholar responded, "No. I don't take my stand on the Word of God; I do all that I can to take my stand underneath the Word of God."

We must do the same. It's under God's Word that we learn God's moral will. And he who stands under God's sovereign will and seeks to know God's moral will has laid the foundation for making wise, prudent, and godly choices.

6

Motivated by Love

On one occasion an expert in the law stood up to test Jesus. "Teacher," he asked, "what must I do to inherit eternal life?"

"What is written in the Law?" he replied. "How do you read it?"

He answered: " 'Love the Lord your God with all your heart and with all your soul and with all your strength and with all your mind' "; and, " 'Love your neighbor as yourself.' "

"You have answered correctly," Jesus replied. "Do this and you will live."

(Luke 10:25–28)

Decision-making can be very difficult. For some of us, it can be almost impossible. We're afraid of decisions; and we back away from them for two reasons.

One reason for our reluctance to make decisions is that we're aware of the consequences. The 1981 film *Chariots of Fire* focused on decisions and their consequences. The film's main character, Eric Liddell, was a Scottish Presbyterian minister who believed that Sunday was the Lord's Day and should be kept sacred. Liddell was also a brilliant athlete, and he qualified to compete in the 1924 Olympics. For years, he had his heart set on running in the games. He knew he had a chance to win a coveted gold medal for England.

But Liddell was in for a surprise. For the first time in history, some Olympic events were scheduled on Sunday—including the contest in which Eric Liddell was to compete. Forced to choose between a potential medal and his principle, he decided to come down on the side of faith.

In one of the film's decisive scenes, Harold Abrahams, a Jewish athlete friend, asked Liddell, "Do you have any regrets?" Eric Liddell responded, "Regrets, yes. Doubts, no."

We often shy away from making such decisions, uncertain that we can handle the regrets. The path we ought to take may be clear-cut, but so are the consequences. It's difficult to choose the path when we do not like where it leads.

But there's a second reason that making decisions is difficult. We often face a decision with uncertain consequences. Not knowing how things will turn out, we are reluctant to decide. We stand at the crossroads and consider the paths before us. We're aware that each path will lead us in a different direction, but we can't be sure where.

Some people decide not to decide. But if we wait for a 20/20 vision of the future, we'll never decide. We will stand immobilized at the point of decision, and instead of making up our minds, circumstances will control our lives. We will have abdicated responsibility.

Whether we are faced with decisions whose consequences are clear, or those in which the consequences remain vague and uncertain, decision-making can be agonizing. Following God's principles for making decisions may make them clearer but the consequences may still be hard, and the uncertainty may continue to be great.

We've considered the need to make decisions in submission to the sovereign will of God. We also discussed making our decisions in submission to God's moral will. These two principles are foundational and will often lighten our load.

But when it comes to decisions that are not clearly spelled out in the Bible, we face new challenges. Many of life's choices are not clearly related to God's moral will. What principles, then, do Christians use when submission to God's sovereign and moral will doesn't provide direction?

The Law of Love

The Bible tells us again and again that love is the motive key to fulfilling God's will. In at least eight separate places, we are told to love God and love our neighbors.

In Luke, a lawyer questioned Jesus, " 'What must I do to inherit eternal life?' 'What is written in the Law?' [Jesus] replied. 'How do you read it?' [The lawyer] answered: " 'Love the Lord your God with all your heart and with all your soul and with all your strength and with all your mind' "; and, " 'Love your neighbor as yourself.' " 'You have answered correctly,' Jesus replied" (Luke 10:25–28). (Jesus gives the lawyer an "A" on the exam.)

"Love is the fulfillment of the law," wrote Paul (Romans 13:10). Love, he said, is the fruit of the Spirit (Galatians 5:22). When it comes to decisions that are not clearly dealt with in the Scriptures, we are to decide on the basis of love.

Following this principle in our culture is difficult—the meaning of love is up for grabs. We hear people say, "I just love strawberries, but they give me a rash." We see "love" on the marquee of the X-rated movie theater, *Love in the Raw*.

Irish playwright George Bernard Shaw once asked, "When you look for deeds done in the name of love, where do you look?" His answer was, "In the murder columns of newspapers."

In our culture, love is considered a strong emotion. Of course, it is legitimate to think of love as a feeling. For those who have fallen in love, it is an overwhelming feeling. We sometimes feel that we have no control over this kind of love.

A mother who has spent months eagerly looking forward to the birth of her baby has no trouble expressing love. When that infant is finally brought to her, the nurse doesn't say, "Now let me teach you how to love your baby." In fact, one Canadian researcher says that when an infant is brought to its mother, a biochemical change actually takes place in the mother, causing her to bond with her baby. She is gripped by an overwhelming emotion as she embraces the child.

Grasping Agape

Neither of these models of love—neither the passion of lovers nor the mother's strong attraction to her newborn—

describes the love God wants us to display. God calls us to an agape love.

In the ancient world, *agape* was a weak, anemic word. It could be translated "good will." But the New Testament writers took that word and filled it with meaning; no longer did it refer primarily to an emotion, but it came to represent a set of the mind, an act of the will. That's why Jesus said, "Love your enemies and pray for those who persecute you" (Matthew 5:44).

The philosopher Immanuel Kant read Jesus' words and dismissed them as impossible. "You cannot command love," he said. And he was right, if Jesus were talking about an emotional love. We cannot command our feelings as we can light a candle or blow out a match. But Jesus wasn't talking about feelings. Jesus was saying that when we deal with anyone, whether friend or foe, we are to seek that person's highest good. We must put another person's interests before our own.

Paul echoed Christ's command when he said, "Each of you should look not only to your own interests, but also to the interests of others" (Philippians 2:4). And, in writing to the Corinthians, he said, "Nobody should seek his own good, but the good of others" (1 Corinthians 10:24).

Agape love is an act of the will in which we put another person's interests before our own. This means that making a decision is more than simply looking at the bottom line. An important part of every decision we make is our motives as they relate to the welfare of others.

Wrong and Right in Black and White

No matter what the consequences—known or unknown—there are some actions that the Bible declares are always wrong.

It is always wrong to commit adultery. It is always wrong to steal. It is always wrong to bear false witness. And it is always wrong to worship idols. These issues are black and white; they are wrong and no motive can turn evil into good.

But interestingly enough, there is no action in the Bible that is ever declared in itself to be right. Good deeds must flow from good motives or they are not good. For example, it is a good thing to pray, but even prayer can be corrupted by bad motives. A Pharisee who stood to pray so that men would hear his prayer was condemned by Jesus (Matthew 6:5). One Sabbath, two men went to the temple to pray. One was a tax collector, and the other, a Pharisee. Both of them prayed, but only one of them went back to his home justified (Luke 18:10–14). Right deeds are righteous only if they proceed from right motives.

Any number of actions, in and of themselves, are neither right nor wrong. They are made right when we act in love. They become wrong if we act in selfishness.

It's like playing the piano. There are no right or wrong notes. There are only right or wrong notes in the context of the musical score. We may not like G or F, or be very fond of middle C, but the note is wrong only in the context of what is being played. Likewise, choices become right or wrong based on the motivation behind them.

Motivation: Love of God

Agape love calls me to seek what benefits others, not merely what benefits me. As I make choices I must also ask, does this choice honor God? Am I pursuing God's interests?

What would life be like if more Christians put this kind of love into action within the church? Paul probably wondered the same thing as he wrote to the quarreling Corinthians. (People who wistfully want to go back to the first-century church, should take another look at 1–2 Corinthians. Is this Corinthian church the idyllic church they want to get back to?)

The Corinthian church was ripped apart by divisions, and people in the church were embroiled in business disputes. They brought their disputes to the secular courts to be tried before a pagan judge in front of a non-Christian audience. As a result, the name of God was smeared among the Gentiles in the city.

This is essentially what Paul said to the people in that less-than-perfect church: "Look, there are people in the church who could have decided that for you. But even if no capable person were found, wouldn't it have been better to have been defrauded and suffer loss than to take your argument to a pagan court and dishonor the name of God?"

The Bottom Line Below the Bottom Line

Some decisions are more important than the mere bottom line. Some things outweigh our petty calculations of personal profit and loss. What Paul is telling us is that a church should sometimes surrender its property rather than to do battle in a secular court. To defame the name of God in an effort to keep property is a wrong decision.

At every point of decision, each of us must ask, "Is God honored in my choice?" And when our choice affects others— who, like us, are made in the image of God—we must make our decision in love.

My wife and I have had to make some hard decisions with regard to aging parents. The moral will of God is clear.

The Ten Commandments say that we are to honor our father and our mother. And Paul wrote in 1 Timothy 5:8 that if anyone does not provide for his relatives, especially those of his immediate family, he has denied the faith. But our decisions were still difficult.

My father, who had been living in one of the toughest neighborhoods of New York City was getting older and weaker. He was also falling victim to that city's renowned violence. In fact, in just two years he had been beaten up twice by thugs. When I found out about it, I went to New York and brought my father back to Dallas, where we lived. I've often said that's the worst decision I could have made. Unfortunately, at that time, it was the *only* decision I could have made.

After he came to live with us, his personality changed. He had always been a kind, gentle man, but he soon became angry and hostile. He'd get up in the middle of the night and wander through the house, coming into our bedroom or our children's. He'd turn on the lights and wake us up. We had to have somebody with him all the time. After three or four months of this, we decided to put my father in a nursing home. We felt that for the sake of our children and our family—even for his sake—it was the best decision to make.

He stayed in that nursing home for eight years. It cost about one-third of my salary each month to keep him there. I doubt that there were more than one or two days in eight years that I failed to visit him when I was in town. And I doubt that there were one or two days in all the times I went to visit him that I felt good about the decision to place him there.

My dad did not like the nursing home and I did not want him to be there. I would leave feeling guilty, wishing I could do something else, but not knowing what else I could do. But as best I knew, I'd done what was best for my father, for my children, and for our home. It was a decision made in love; it was a tough decision and it never became easy.

After my father died, we moved to Denver. The first week we were in Colorado, my wife's mother suffered a fall in Oregon. Bonnie went to be with her, and while she was there her mother discovered that she had cancer. It was cancer that had caused the fall that resulted in a broken leg.

We decided that the only thing we could do was to bring Bonnie's mother back to Denver. We sold her house and brought her—along with her possessions—to live with us.

After she had lived with us for about three months, a nursing home opened in our community. I urged my wife to put her mother in the home, knowing it was a strain for her to take care of her mother. But after thinking and praying about it, Bonnie determined that her mother would get better care in our home than she would in a nursing home. For eighteen months Mrs. Vick lived with us; then she died of cancer. The entire time she was with us she did not get out of bed, and my wife had to give her constant attention.

It was a difficult time in our marriage; in fact, the most difficult time we had ever experienced. Here we were in a new ministry—living with a mother who needed care day and night. But we were convinced that it was the loving thing to do.

As far as I know, we made both of these decisions in love. We wanted what was best for our parents. But they were not the only ones involved. Everyone in the situation had to be considered. They were agonizing decisions but we tried our best to ensure that the motive behind them was love. And that made the decisions easier on us.

Many people don't want to make good decisions, they want to make painless decisions. There are many painless decisions in life and God's principles help with those. But God never promised that making godly decisions would be easy. Many of life's toughest decisions cause us agony and frustration; it seems that there's no easy choice. In these cases, God's principle of making decisions based on a motive of love for others helps us to know we are doing what God wants us to do.

7

Knowing Your Strengths

Just as each of us has one body with many members, and these members do not all have the same function, so in Christ we who are many form one body, and each member belongs to all the others. We have different gifts, according to the grace given us. If a man's gift is prophesying, let him use it in proportion to his faith. If it is serving, let him serve; if it is teaching, let him teach; if it is encouraging, let him encourage; if it is contributing to the needs of others, let him give generously; if it is leadership, let him govern diligently; if it is showing mercy, let him do it cheerfully.

(Romans 12:4–8)

So far, all of the biblical principles for decision-making have focused on godly attitudes. First there was submission to the sovereign will of God, then submission to the moral will of God. Next we looked at making decisions based on the motive of love and seeking the best for others.

But now it's time for some personal analysis. The Bible teaches that godly decision-making requires knowing our strengths and then exercising those strengths.

That's what Paul was getting at when he wrote, "I urge you, brothers, in view of God's mercy, to offer your bodies as living sacrifices, holy and pleasing to God—this is your spiritual act of worship. Do not conform any longer to the pattern of this world, but be transformed by the renewing of your mind. Then you will be able to test and approve what God's will is—his good, pleasing and perfect will" (Romans 12:1–2).

Paul touched on a number of points in this brief passage. First is his admonition to submit ourselves to God. Second, we are encouraged to stop allowing our society to pour us into its mold. Instead, we are to be transformed by the renewing of our minds. We can't know ourselves or glorify God if we're merely acting on impulses that have been formed by our social environment.

In the rest of this epistle, Paul spelled out how we are to think. It is not some kind of mystical infusion of divine insight that transforms the mind. Instead, Paul called for a radical reorganization of one's approach to life.

First of all, Paul advocates a realistic self-evaluation. "By the grace given me I say to every one of you: Do not think of yourself more highly than you ought, but rather think of yourself with sober judgment, in accordance with the measure of faith God has given you" (12:3). The phrase *the measure of faith* means the spiritual gift given us because of our faith.

We need to be sober in our judgment of our gifts and talents. Paul's message is urgent: We ought to know ourselves; we ought to know our strengths; and we ought to know our weaknesses. We shouldn't think more highly of ourselves than we ought to think, nor should we put ourselves down.

Know Thyself!

Have you ever had a friend who seemed to know you better than you knew yourself? Wise are the people who listen to a friend's evaluation of their abilities.

Sometimes taking a personality test like the MMPI (Minnesota Multiphasic Personality Inventory) or the Taylor-Johnson Temperamental Analysis can give you insight into the kind of person you are. Tests like these have helped me learn more about my own personality and leadership style. Whatever the method, a sober evaluation of our talents enables us to make better choices.

But then, having understood what our gifts and abilities are, we need to go with our strengths. According to Paul, everyone is gifted differently—and all gifts are needed:

Just as each of us has one body with many members, and these members do not all have the same function, so in Christ we who are many form one body, and each member belongs to all the others. We have different gifts, according to the grace given us. If a man's gift is prophesying, let him use it in proportion to his faith. If it is serving, let him serve; if it is teaching, let him teach; if it is encouraging, let him encourage; if it is contributing to the needs of others, let him give generously; if it is leadership, let him govern diligently; if it is showing mercy, let him do it cheerfully. (12:4–8)

Paul resembles a proud parent standing on the sidelines yelling, "Go with your strength! Go with your strength!"

Focusing on Our Weaknesses

Unfortunately, we don't always do that. Often we have a strange fascination with our weaknesses. Perhaps we pay more attention to our weaknesses because we're insecure about them. Or maybe our weaknesses are always cropping up in life.

If you've ever taught a communications class, you know that students who stutter often want to become public speakers. I commend them for wanting to deal with the difficulty in their lives, but it may not be the shrewdest decision to choose a career that requires public speaking. We are often wrapped up in our own weaknesses, and we often make choices based on those weaknesses.

Another way we focus on our weaknesses is by accepting excellent opportunities for which we are not prepared. We may have an opportunity to play the church pipe organ, but have abilities commensurate with playing a harmonica. As a result, we easily fall victim to the Peter Principle and rise to the level of our incompetence. We pursue our weaknesses—instead of our strengths—because we see an opportunity. But we fail to ask ourselves if we really have the ability to make the best of that opportunity.

Instead, Paul would say, "Know yourself. Know your abilities. Do what you can to shore up your weaknesses, but go with your strength."

Case Study: The Jerusalem Church

The early church followed Paul's advice. Acts 6 gives us an on-the-scene report of a problem faced by Jerusalem's church leaders. The church had among its members a number of Greek-speaking widows. These women lived in an Aramaic-speaking community and when it came to the distribution of goods, they felt they weren't getting their fair share. The widows formed a grievance committee; they were upset and they let everybody know it. What began as a social-cultural problem rapidly became a spiritual problem. The apostles were confronted with a crucial decision.

It is interesting to note that Acts doesn't say the leaders fell on their faces waiting for God to give them a solution to their problem. They had to make a decision, and the decision they made was a wise one.

They didn't say, "This is a great opportunity for us to model servant leadership. We can go down there and serve those tables." No! We read, "The Twelve gathered all the disciples together and said, 'It would not be right for us to neglect the ministry of the word of God in order to wait on tables. Brothers, choose seven men from among you who are known to be full of the Spirit and wisdom. We will turn this responsibility over to them and will give our attention to prayer and the ministry of the word' " (Acts 6:2–4).

The apostles set the qualifications for a committee to take over this responsibility: They had to be spiritual men, know how to handle life skillfully, and have the respect of the church. Something else we should notice—all seven men chosen were probably Greeks. That was shrewd. Since the Greek-speaking widows were upset, the church chose Greek-speaking men to make the decisions. This solution left the apostles free to minister the Word of God and to pray.

Choose Others for Their Strengths

Wise decisions come when you consider your strengths and the strengths of others and build on those strengths. If you were in charge of finding an accountant for a Christian organization, you would not hire me. When it comes to balancing my checkbook, if I come within two or three dollars, I assume that the bank is always right and I settle for that. If I were keeping books for a business and saw that we were a couple of dollars short in balancing them, I'd throw in what we lacked and call it quits for the day. Accountants are very, very picky. They insist that the books in a business have to be balanced exactly.

I think I have a reasonably good spiritual life and I'm honest. But those would not be the only characteristics you would look for in an accountant. You need someone who knows the methods of accounting. The apostles went with their strengths, and they trusted the strengths of others. In doing so, they made a wise decision.

Know your strength, and then go with your strength. That's crucial in making good personal decisions. And remember that each of us has different strengths to bring to the different situations we face.

Different Gifts, Different Strengths

A concert violinist had a brother who was a bricklayer. One day a woman gushed to the bricklayer, "It must be wonderful to be in a family with such a famous violinist." Then, not wanting to insult the bricklayer she said, "Of course we don't all have the same talents, and even in a family, some just seem to have more talent than others."

The bricklayer said, "Boy, you're telling me! That violinist brother of mine doesn't know a thing about laying bricks. And if he couldn't make some money playing that fiddle of his, he couldn't hire a guy with know-how like mine to build a house. If he had to build a house himself he'd be ruined."

If you want to build a house, you don't want a violinist. And if you're going to lead an orchestra, you don't want a bricklayer.

No two of us are exactly alike. None of us has every gift and ability. Each of us has a responsibility to exercise the gifts we have—not the ones we wish we had.

And when it comes to making decisions about your own life and the direction it should take, focus on your strengths—not your weaknesses. Know yourself. Know what you do well, and then go with your strengths and shore up your weaknesses.

8

Considering the Circumstances

When the islanders saw the snake hanging from [Paul's] hand, they said to each other, "This man must be a murderer; for though he escaped from the sea, Justice has not allowed him to live." But Paul shook the snake off into the fire and suffered no ill effects. The people expected him to swell up or suddenly fall dead, but after waiting a long time and seeing nothing unusual happen to him, they changed their minds and said he was a god.

(Acts 28:4–6)

The opening chapter of the Bible tells us that men and women are made in the image of God (Genesis 1:27). That great declaration is repeated twice more in the first book of the Bible alone (5:1; 9:6).

Across the centuries, theologians have wrestled with what the Scriptures mean when they say "made in the image of God." Thomas Aquinas, a significant theologian and a pioneer in Catholic thought, believed that the image of God referred to our ability to reason. Scientists evidently felt that Thomas Aquinas was on to something, because the scientific name given to mankind is *homo sapiens,* that is, the creatures *(homo)* who think and reason *(sapia).*

This is one of the qualities that distinguishes people from animals. We do not survive because of physical strength, or because of superior instinct, but because of our capacity to think and reason. Whatever else is inferred by the image of God, certainly part of it is the ability to think, to choose, to aspire, to hope, and—as we are examining—to decide. In that is the glory, and in that is the tension.

We must take advantage of the freedom that God gives us, and we must be aware that in that freedom there is responsibility. What is more, as Christians, we are to make our decisions in a way that God wants us to make them. We are to think God's thoughts after Him.

As we have seen, the Bible gives us principles to use as we come to the decisions of life. We must submit to God's sovereign and moral will. We must make our decisions based on the motive of love, seeking the best for others. We must also use our God-given intelligence to become aware of our strengths and weaknesses.

The fifth principle of biblical decision-making involves considering the circumstances surrounding a decision.

Lack of Circumstantial Evidence

Many people overemphasize the importance of circumstances in the decision-making process. Although circumstances are a factor in nearly all decisions, it is important to avoid letting circumstances dictate the decisions we make.

Many people consider circumstances to be God's voice—they depend on circumstantial evidence. But circumstances are simply the factors that bring us to the point of decision. They often outline the decision that must be made, but circumstances in themselves are not necessarily signs of God's guidance.

I'm reminded of the Rorschach Test, the psychological test featuring the big inkblots. Psychologists ask their clients to describe what they see in the blots. One person may see a beautiful butterfly. Another sees, in the same blots, demons coming to claim his soul. Circumstances often work the same way. The way we interpret events in our lives often reveals more about our innermost hearts than our outward circumstances.

Circumstances don't provide us with the guidance we need to make good decisions. If we try to figure out what God is doing in our circumstances, we will often come away more confused than informed. We see this truth in a humorous incident recorded in the final chapter of the book of Acts.

Paul and his physician friend, Luke, were shipwrecked and washed ashore on the island of Malta. To keep warm, Paul gathered some sticks. As he put his bundle on the fire, a viper sank its fangs into the flesh of his hand. When the people of Malta saw what happened, they interpreted the circumstance in light of God's providence: "This man must be a murderer; for though he escaped from the sea, Justice has not allowed him to live" (Acts 28:4).

But Paul shook off the viper into the fire, and its poison apparently had no effect. When the people saw this new set of circumstances, they completely reversed themselves. Acts tells us, "They changed their minds and said he was a god" (28:6).

In both cases, these people were doing their very best to read the circumstances. And in both cases, they were wrong!

"Where Are We Going and Why?"

Look at how difficult it would have been to determine God's will in the events surrounding Jesus' birth.

In the account in Luke 2 that is so much a part of the Christmas story, we learn that a decree went out from Caesar Augustus that all the world should be taxed. As a result, everyone had to go back to his birthplace to register for the taxes.

Mary and Joseph traveled from Nazareth in the north down to Bethlehem in the south. But let's imagine that, at the same time, down in Jerusalem, there is another couple named Samuel and Martha. Samuel and Martha are devout people, like Mary and Joseph, and they too have to enroll for the tax. Since Samuel grew up in Galilee in the town of Capernaum, he and his wife have to make the journey north.

Imagine also that Samuel and Martha are along in years, and Martha has just gotten over a bad case of the flu. This new imperial decree comes at the worst possible time. Imagine Martha saying to her husband, "Why in the world would this happen to us now?" Perhaps her husband might reason, "Well, Martha, God has His purposes and maybe as we travel up to Capernaum we'll find someone God wants us to minister to. Or someone up in Capernaum may need our help, and that's why we must make this journey."

And so they go up to Capernaum, they enroll, and they return home again. Along the way they may not have been able to demonstrate their faith or help anybody in need.

But, unbeknownst to Samuel and Martha, God was at work in the circumstances. God wanted to get Joseph and Mary from Nazareth down to Bethlehem, to fulfill prophecy. And to do it, He used circumstances that unsettled people throughout the ancient world.

When Roman officials made that decree, they didn't know they were acting under God's supervision. And hundreds of devout people like Martha and Samuel were probably bewildered as they tried to read God's purposes into all that was happening.

The struggles of Joseph and Mary—along with these of our fictional friends, Samuel and Martha—point out that you cannot know, or even confirm, God's will by trying to decipher circumstances.

Christ's Confounding Birth

If ever a couple was in the will of God, it was Mary and Joseph. An angel appeared to Mary and announced that the child in her womb had been placed there by God. Then, the angel appeared to Joseph in a dream to assure him that he ought to take Mary as his wife. Mary and

Joseph knew that God was working in a mysterious way in their lives.

But as they left Nazareth and traveled down to Bethlehem, they might have begun to wonder what God was doing. When they got to Bethlehem, the town was crowded. No room was available in the caravansary, the place where poor people stayed. So Joseph and Mary had to find a less desirable spot, and Mary gave birth to her son and placed Him in a manger.

We romanticize the manger scene so much that we lose sight of how disturbing it must have been for Mary and Joseph. If we can get past the Christmas cards—past all the hazy pictures of Mary, Joseph, the baby, the shepherds, and the wise men lined up for a family portrait—then we can recognize that the terrifying element in bringing one's firstborn into the world in a village far from home. We would not glamorize or romanticize having to put a newborn in a manger—especially when the only other option was the filthy floor of a cattle shed.

Scripture tells us that Mary pondered these things in her heart. I suspect that she was not as questioning as I. If I had been Mary, I think I would have grumbled to Joseph, "You know, if God has planned this event from the foundation of the world, you'd think He could have reserved a room for us! If we're in God's will, why are we out here in this dingy cave?"

The answer—and I believe Mary saw this—is that you cannot confirm God's will by looking at circumstances. By reading circumstances, you do not necessarily understand the workings of God. Sometimes you might as well read tea leaves.

Does God Root for the Home Team?

The temptation to equate God's will with favorable circumstances is especially tempting in win-lose situations. Whether a big game for our hometown baseball team, or the ebb and flow of warfare as our country's soldiers fight a battle on foreign soil, we tend to think that God favored the winner and opposed the loser. It's certainly an understandable conclusion, but one that's unreliable and ill-advised.

When I lived in Dallas I came under the influence of a Dallas Cowboys football mania that seemed to have the entire city in its grip. Everyone believed that the Cowboys were God's team; some even claimed that the hole in the roof of Texas Stadium was there so God could see His team play.

Back in the 1970s, the Dallas Cowboys played the Minnesota Vikings in a hotly contested play-off game. In the game's closing seconds—with Dallas behind—Cowboy quarterback Roger Staubach threw a "Hail Mary" pass. Essentially, a "Hail Mary" pass means the quarterback flings the ball the length of the field and prays that somebody on his team will catch it in the end zone. In this case, Cowboy receiver Drew Pearson caught Staubach's desperation pass, stepped over the goal line, and the Cowboys won the game. It was one of the greatest triumphs in history if you're a Cowboy fan—or a great disaster if you happen to root for the Vikings.

A day or so after the game, a woman of obviously pious disposition wrote to the Minneapolis paper saying that the reason that the Vikings lost was obvious. Sunday is the Lord's Day, she said, and everybody should remember the Sabbath Day to keep it holy. God must be punishing the Vikings for playing football on Sunday.

The editors could not resist a satirical response, "We would like to inform the reader that the Cowboys—who happened to win the game—played the game on Sunday, too."

Interpreting Calamities

It's very hard to read the providence of God from circumstances. Many continue to attribute to God's will some of the horrible calamities that occur throughout the world. Whenever there is an earthquake or other natural disaster, some religious type is sure this is the wrath of God.

In 1906 an earthquake virtually destroyed the city of San Francisco. San Francisco has always existed on the edge of morality—some would say it has fallen over the edge. When that great earthquake came, many preachers in this country declared that the destruction of San Francisco was the righteous judgment of God.

A cynical poet questioned the assumption. "If, as they say, God sank the town for being overly frisky, why did He burn down the churches and leave standing Hotling's whiskey?"

We don't have the mind of God. As Paul said, "We see through a glass darkly." Therefore, it's impossible for us to look at a set of circumstances and determine from those circumstances the will of God.

Paul Confronts Circumstances

Circumstances aren't like big tea leaves that reveal the hidden will of God, but circumstances often do outline for us the boundaries of our decision.

We see this reflected in many circumstances reported in the book of Acts. Paul was faced with several different circumstances, and in each situation he has to make choices. It will be helpful for us to look at the decisions he made.

Escaping from the Assassins

In Acts 9, we discover that after Paul's encounter with Christ on the Damascus Road, he continued on into the city. Once in Damascus, some of the Christians cared for him. But some Jews who found out what had happened were upset that Paul had let the Jewish team down. Acting on their anger, they hired some hit-men to assassinate the new apostle. These assassins positioned themselves at the gates of the city and watched for Paul's departure.

When Paul and his new followers discovered that the gates were being watched by assassins, they decided to do something about it. The Christians secretly lowered Paul down in a basket over the side of the wall in the middle of the night.

Paul didn't say, "Look, God encountered me on the Damascus Road, and I know He has a mission for me to perform so I must be invincible." Instead, faced with a very dangerous set of circumstances, everyone used common sense. And Paul fled the city.

Demanding an Honor Guard Escort

An entirely different set of circumstances confronted Paul in Acts 16:19–40. Paul had landed in the city of Philippi, where he and Silas were arrested for disturbing the peace. Before they were thrown into jail, the Romans flogged them. The next morning, the Roman officials discovered that they had made a terrible mistake. They had failed to check the passports and hadn't realized that Paul was a Roman citizen. All the laws and customs said that no one could flog Roman citizens, and so, the Roman leaders asked Paul to leave Philippi quietly.

But Paul refused to sneak out of town. This time he demanded an honor guard to escort him through the center of the city. Paul knew that Philippi was a Roman outpost, and many who lived there were retired Roman leaders; and one way to bring dignity and attention to the new cause of Christ was to have an honor guard through the city. This time Paul left with a flourish.

Avoiding Assassins Again

In Acts 20:1–3, Paul was in Greece and planned to travel to Syria when he discovered that a group of Jews had plotted to kill him. Again, Paul didn't say, "Well, I'm in God's sovereign will and I know He wants me to go to Syria; therefore, no one can touch me." Instead, he changed his travel plans. His sea voyage abandoned, Paul went north by land. He traveled to Philippi and visited a number of other cities until the plot against him had died out. And then he proceeded upon his way.

So we can see from the life of Paul that circumstances were—at best—difficult to read. And certainly, they didn't determine the course Paul took. Three separate times Paul was confronted with danger. Once he fled. Once he stayed. Once he avoided the problem. Paul made decisions. He did not allow his decisions to be made by the circumstances.

Open Doors

These three incidents involve negative circumstances. In three separate sets of dangerous circumstances, Paul made three different decisions. But the principle of not letting circumstances determine our decisions applies to positive incidents as well. An "open door" is not necessarily the finger of God pointing and telling you to forge ahead at double speed.

The phrase *open door* is used five times in the New Testament: Acts 14:27, 1 Corinthians 16:9, 2 Corinthians 2:12, Colossians 4:3, and Revelation 3:8. In each instance it refers to an opportunity, generally a ministry opportunity, to serve Jesus Christ. Usually, when there was an open door, the apostles entered it—but not always.

Look at Paul's response to two interesting sets of circumstances recorded in his Corinthian correspondence.

Paul wrote to the believers in Corinth: "I do not want to see you now and make only a passing visit; I hope to spend some time with you, if the Lord permits. But I will stay on at Ephesus until Pentecost, because a great door for effective work has opened to me, and there are many who oppose me" (1 Corinthians 16:7–9).

Paul explained that he was staying at Ephesus. Opportunities had opened, and apparently, he felt that by staying at Ephesus he may have become able to minimize opposition against his ministry. Paul saw an open door at Ephesus and he took advantage of the opportunity; he stayed.

But in 2 Corinthians, Paul referred to another open door: "When I went to Troas to preach the gospel of Christ and found that the Lord had opened a door for me, I still had no peace of mind, because I did not find my brother Titus there. So I said good-by to them and went on to Macedonia" (2 Corinthians 2:12–13).

Here's a little background on what was going on with the Corinthians. Paul loved that congregation dearly, but when he had heard that some of them were not walking according to the truth, he wrote them a severe letter. Not knowing how they would act, he worried.

Paul had arranged with Titus to meet him at Troas to find out about the Corinthians' response. But Titus missed his connection and, for some reason, didn't show up. And Paul, because he was troubled about what had transpired at Corinth, decided to go on to Macedonia to learn there how the Corinthians had reacted to his letter.

Now, if an open door determines the direction of God, then what Paul did is absolutely bewildering. He had an open door, but went in a completely different direction. But if an open door is simply a circumstance to be evaluated according to one's priorities in life—including the priority Paul placed on reducing his own inner turmoil—then Paul was free to make a choice. He made his decision based on what he considered most important. And he turned away from the open door.

An open door is not necessarily the guidance of God. It is simply one of a number of alternatives to be considered.

His Ways Are Not Our Ways

Don't misunderstand. I am not saying that God does not work in and through our circumstances. Certainly He does. But we're not always aware of how God is working. And the fact that God is at work in our lives doesn't remove our ever-present responsibility to make decisions.

In the opening verses of Romans, Paul tells the Roman Christians of his desire to visit them. "God, whom I serve with my whole heart in preaching the gospel of his Son, is my witness how constantly I remember you in my prayers at all times; and I pray that now at last by God's will the way may be opened for me to come to you" (Romans 1:9–10).

Paul may have suspected trouble if he were able to go to Rome, the capital of that empire. But I doubt that Paul thought about becoming a prisoner there under house arrest, which is how things ended up for him. I suspect he focused on getting to that great Roman capital and preaching the gospel to the people who flooded through that city, thus dispersing the Good News throughout the ancient world.

It took awhile, but Paul arrived in Rome, as a prisoner. He was placed under arrest, chained to a Roman soldier. Paul could have pondered, *Where's God in all of this? I mean, if He wants the Gospel to be proclaimed to Rome, why am I stuck here guarded by these soldiers?* But instead Paul carefully evaluated the circumstances. He realized that while he was chained to a Roman soldier, the Roman soldier was chained to him. And so as the guards came and went, he ministered to each one of them.

Paul, in his letter to the Christians at Philippi, expressed his opinion about how God used the circumstances of his arrest:

> I want you to know, brothers, that what has happened to me has really served to advance the gospel. As a result, it has become clear throughout the whole palace guard and to everyone else that I am in chains for Christ. Because of my chains, most of the brothers in the Lord have been encouraged to speak the word of God more courageously and fearlessly. (Philippians 1:12–14)

In those unpleasant circumstances, Paul kept on with his ministry. He didn't allow circumstances to silence him, nor his chains to determine whether he was in or out of the will of God.

Later, Paul was freed and evidently went back to Rome. This time he was not under house arrest; he lingered in a dungeon facing execution. But he remained true to his mission regardless of the circumstances.

Unfortunately, that wasn't the case for Demas, a one-time associate of Paul's. Paul wrote, "Demas, because he loved this world, has deserted me and has gone to Thessalonica" (2 Timothy 4:10). Demas, it seems, had looked at the circumstances and decided to check out. As a result, he earned a place in the pages of Scripture as a deserter and a coward.

But Paul, whether under house arrest or in a dungeon in Rome, continued his ministry. It is there that he wrote to the churches that he cared about and to his dear comrades. It is his writings from Rome, written under dismal circumstances, that form the core of the New Testament letters that have been read for two thousand years.

Many of these letters were written under the worst possible circumstances in a prison cell, chained to a soldier. But God worked in and through those circumstances, and the entire church was edified.

Circumstances, whether good or bad, do not determine the will of God. They often bring us to the point of decision, but we must still decide and carry out our own predetermined spiritual priorities. Circumstances must be weighed if we are to make good decisions, but they shouldn't be given more emphasis than they deserve.

٩

Seeking Godly Counsel

Listen to advice and accept instruction, and in the end you will be wise.

(Proverbs 19:20)

While I was president of Denver Seminary, the seminary was brought to the point of a major of decision. We were presented with a proposal to move to a larger campus in a different area of town. Every silver lining has its cloud, and while there were many advantages to the move, certain disadvantages were also apparent.

The faculty was deeply involved in the decision, and I did my best to lay out the benefits and disadvantages of the proposal. After we discussed it, I suggested that each faculty member take a week to think about it, pray about it for fifteen minutes each day, and then regroup at the end of the week to make a decision.

I believe the faculty was made up of spiritual people, people who know the Bible. And certainly, they were individuals who wanted what was best for the seminary and for the student body. I was expecting a strong sense of direction when we gathered to make our decision.

But when this group of eighteen mature, thoughtful, Christian men and women came back together, the unexpected occurred. The vote was nine in favor of the move; nine opposed.

At one time in my life that vote would have deeply disturbed me. After all, if God is the Lord of this seminary, and we look to Him to know His will, and we ask Him to speak, then can't we expect Him to speak with an unambiguous voice? But what do we do with a nine-to-nine deadlock? Has God in His wisdom spoken to the one group while hiding His will from the others? If that's the case, which nine heard His voice?

Or perhaps God spoke clearly to all eighteen, and nine were disobedient to the heavenly voice! Depending on our theology, we can come away from such a vote with a number of questions and a great deal of turmoil.

If in that decision about moving the seminary we had been asking the question, "How do we know God's will?" we would have emerged from that split-vote feeling uncertain and confused. But as we have seen, asking how to know God's will is not a biblical question. Instead, we are better off asking, "How do we make good decisions?" In our case, the fact that we were evenly split led to our decision not to move our campus.

If we change the question, we change the direction of our answer. And when the focus comes back on us and on making godly decisions, we need to follow God's principles for decision-making. Here are the five principles we've covered so far:

1. Make decisions in submission to God's sovereign will.
2. Make decisions in submission to God's moral will.
3. Make love and concern for the good of others the motive.
4. Focus on your strengths and gifts.
5. Consider the circumstances, but don't be mastered by them.

Making good decisions is seldom easy. A recent seminary graduate called me and told me that he and his wife had decided to look into an opportunity for ministry in another state. In fact, they had gone further than that; they had made up their minds to go. But just as they had reached a point of decision, another opportunity opened up in another part of the country. Now they were faced with two opportunities.

The first question this young man asked me was, "What do you think God's trying to tell us?" I hear that question often, and the fact is that I don't ever know how to answer—it's not a valid question. What I told the young minister was this: "You've got two wonderful opportunities before you. What you've got to do is weigh the two alternatives in terms of your spiritual priorities, your personal priorities, and good old common sense, and then make your choice. God may not be telling you anything by giving you two opportunities, but you are responsible to Him to make the best decision you can."

Basing Decisions on Wise Counsel

Although that young man was troubled and confused, he was following the sixth principle of godly decision-making, which is this: We must include wise counsel in the process. The Bible has a great deal to say about seeking out the advice of other people.

As I was writing this I thumbed through the book of Proverbs and picked out six passages urging us to seek counsel. We could find many more, but take a look at these:

> For lack of guidance a nation falls, but many advisers make victory sure. (Proverbs 11:14)
>
> He who walks with the wise grows wise, but a companion of fools suffers harm. (13:20)
>
> Plans fail for lack of counsel, but with many advisers they succeed. (15:22)

Listen to advice and accept instruction, and in the end you will be wise. (19:20)

Make plans by seeking advice; if you wage war, obtain guidance. (20:18)

A wise man has great power, and a man of knowledge increases strength; for waging war you need guidance, and for victory many advisers. (24:5–6)

It is very popular to joke about committees. Someone described a committee as "a group of the unfit appointed by the unwilling to do the unnecessary." Or, "A camel is a horse put together by a committee." But the Bible puts a great deal of emphasis on seeking out wise counsel. And the goal is not only to seek counsel, but to consider what you hear.

Recently, a businessman took a golf pro to a local golf course. It was obvious that the businessman wanted to improve his swing. So he would stand and hit the ball and the golf pro would try to correct his swing, his stance, the direction he looked, and his overall approach to the game. But each time the golf pro tried to correct him, the businessman—who was a successful C.E.O.—kept insisting that the way he was doing it was more comfortable, and in fact better. Before long, the golf pro began agreeing with what the businessman was saying.

A man standing nearby watched this whole scene. Seeing the businessman pay the pro and walk off with a smile, he approached the pro and asked, "What happened? In the middle of that session you just began to tell him what he wanted to hear." The golf pro responded, "You know, I've been at this long enough to know what people want. That man wasn't paying me for counsel; he was just paying for an echo."

If we surround ourselves with people who echo our own opinions, that is not wise, and that is not good counsel. We've seen how leaders, even presidents, have fallen because they were surrounded by yes-men instead of insightful men and women who give thoughtful, unbiased counsel.

Seeking Counsel in Three Areas

All decisions are not the same. Nor is all counsel. When we look for good counsel, we should seek it on several different levels. Here are three important areas of counsel that we should consider in making good decisions:

Biblical Counsel

Many of the decisions we make have spiritual implications. If we know people who are mighty in the Scriptures and who know how to apply the Bible to life, we ought to seek them out to discuss the spiritual implications of our decisions.

A myriad of voices in our culture gives us counsel that is not God's counsel. The psalmist says that we are not to walk in the counsel of the wicked or stand in the way of sinners or sit in the seat of the mockers (Psalm 1:1). I do not think it's wise to accept the counsel of a talk-show host who has been married three times on how to have a good marriage. Newspaper columnists are fun to read but we shouldn't take their counsel seriously as the basis for our important choices. But God says we are wise to turn for advice to people who know the Scriptures and know how to bring them to bear on our decisions.

Experienced Counsel

Here's a second maxim for seeking valuable counsel: Ask those who have gone through similar experiences. The editor of Proverbs spends the first nine chapters urging young people to listen to the advice of older people, especially parents. Those who have lived to a good age and have lived perceptively often give us wise counsel because they've traveled a road that is very similar to the road we are traveling.

There's an old story of a man in West Virginia who had a reputation for being wise and for giving sound advice. A young person went to him one day and asked, "Uncle Jed, how come you have such good judgment?" "Well, I've got good judgment because I've had a lot of experience," he replied. And the boy said, "Yes, but how did you get all that experience?" "Well," he mused, "I got it by making a lot of bad judgments."

If people have traveled the road before us and can tell us what that road looks like, then we are wise to listen to what they have to say.

Let's add one caution about seeking experienced counsel: It's dangerous to rely on just one person's experience. Mark Twain used to tell about a cat who sat on a hot stove lid. That experience taught the cat never to sit on a hot stove lid again. But further, that cat never sat on a cold stove lid either. He took more from the experience than it had to offer. If we're going to talk about experiences, we would be wise to talk with a number of people who have faced similar decisions and extract direction from their combined counsel.

The Best Available Counsel

First seek biblical counsel, then experienced counsel. In some situations, we need the best counsel available, whether or not it is the counsel of Christians.

Let me explain what I mean. Let's say you are trying to decide whether or not you should have cosmetic surgery. The first level of counsel would be to decide whether it is biblical. Are there spiritual dimensions to this surgery? Are you perhaps placing too much emphasis on external appearances for your happiness in life?

You can gain valuable information from people who have had such surgery. Was great pain involved? Did the surgery work? Were its effects lasting? What kinds of side effects did they experience? What surgeon did they choose? How did they make that choice?

But to find the third level of counsel—the best advice possible—you might want to talk with a good plastic surgeon about the proposed operation. The surgeon may not be a Christian, but if he's qualified, he ought to know everything you need to know about the surgery itself.

I have never understood a concept that continues to make the rounds in our country; it's something called, "The Christian Yellow Pages." Could it be that a Christian repairs television sets better than a non-Christian? Does a Christian barber give better haircuts than a non-Christian? If we're looking for an auto mechanic, isn't it better to find one who can fix cars, rather than one whose sole claim to our business is that he has a daily quiet time?

When I was working with the Christian Medical Society, people often asked me to recommend a Christian surgeon. I was always tempted to ask, "Do you want someone who reads the Bible or who reads medical journals?" When it comes to surgery, I want a skilled, capable surgeon; whether he or she has had devotions that morning isn't as essential as whether he or she has been board-certified. At that level, we're not looking for Christian counsel, we're looking for good counsel.

It may seem like a lot of effort to run all our decisions through these three levels of counsel. And if the decision is as mundane as a choice between vanilla and chocolate ice cream, such counsel seeking is obviously unnecessary. But if we're facing an important decision, the three-level approach will help us reach better decisions.

Heed the Counsel You Receive

Even when we have received all the best counsel we can find, we are still responsible for our own decisions. No matter what the advice is and no matter who is giving it to us, we make the final choice, and we are responsible for that choice.

A few years ago, I talked with a woman in her ninth month of pregnancy. She wanted to travel from the east coast to California, but when she asked her obstetrician, he advised against the trip. But she told me, "I just kept nagging at him until he let me go."

Fortunately, the trip turned out all right. But that woman was awarding magical power to the advice of her obstetrician. If his best judgment was that she shouldn't go, it was stupid for her to nag him into changing his mind. Why seek out counsel if you simply want people to agree with what you have already decided to do?

Christians who have already made up their minds about their lifestyle seek out churches and pastors who approve of it. But pastors are not Protestant popes; they do not speak *ex cathedra,* in the power of their office. The best they can do is to counsel according to the Scriptures and their experience. But to seek out people until we find someone who agrees with us is folly.

Paul wrote Timothy to warn him that "the time will come when men will not put up with sound doctrine. Instead, to suit their own desires, they will gather around them a great number of teachers to say what their itching ears want to hear" (2 Timothy 4:3). Such people turn their ears away from truth and turn aside to myth. False teachers will be judged, but people who seek out false teachers will be losers as well.

We need to seek out good counsel, but no counselor can make the decision for us. We are responsible for weighing the counsel and for making the choices.

10

The Place of Revelation

"Not everyone who says to me, 'Lord, Lord,' will enter the kingdom of heaven, but only he who does the will of my Father who is in heaven. Many will say to me on that day, 'Lord, Lord, did we not prophesy in your name, and in your name drive out demons and perform many miracles?' Then I will tell them plainly, 'I never knew you. Away from me, you evildoers!' "

(Matthew 7:21–23)

Our final principle grows out of the pervasive question, "Don't you think that God could give us special revelation? Can't God speak to us directly, apart from His Word? Can't God give to His people today the kind of spectacular revelations that He gave in Bible times?"

It is presumptuous to decide what God can and cannot do. God can do anything He pleases, even if it contradicts everything I've said. But what God can do and what God does do are two separate things. The answer to that question is yes, I think that God can—and sometimes does—give special revelation to His people. And I think that this can happen even today.

But, having said that, I think that seeking God's special revelation is generally the least effective method of discerning God's will. That's why I have placed it last. It is clear that God's major way of speaking to His people today is through His Word.

That does not put us at a disadvantage. It doesn't mean that back in the good old days of the first century, or the Old Testament, God was alive and vital, but now we are stuck with a dusty old book. It doesn't mean that God has died, or that our lives and our world are barren of His intervention. Far from it. The Bible is God's living Word. He has given it to us. And in some ways we have advantages over God's people in days gone by because the Scriptures are completely sufficient to give us all we need, for all life's situations, to be all that God wants us to be.

When God Speaks

God may sometimes speak directly to us, but that doesn't mean He speaks constantly to each of us like some kind of celestial busybody.

When does God speak? It's interesting that when we study the book of Acts, we see God's special revelation comes to the apostles, and to other Christians, when they aren't even looking for it.

In Acts 8, Philip was ministering up in Samaria, evidently with great success. An angel of God appeared to him and sent him down to the Gaza Strip to talk to an Ethiopian eunuch. The angel did not counsel Philip as he knelt before God wondering what to do next. Instead, Philip was interrupted in the middle of his ministry. And Philip dropped what he was doing, moved out of Samaria, and found the eunuch over in Gaza.

In Acts 10, God brought His special message to two servants simultaneously. An angel came to Cornelius and told him to send for Peter. Meanwhile over in Joppa, the Spirit told Peter to go with the men sent by Cornelius to fetch him. As far as we know, neither Cornelius nor Peter was seeking such divine direction. But God was making a major turn in opening the Gospel to the Gentiles, and, as a result, provided special revelation.

We get a similar example of God's intervention in Acts 16 where Luke reported the vision of a man from Macedonia. Paul had made one tour of duty through Asia Minor and he planned to go east again. But the Spirit stopped him and told Paul in a vision to go to Greece. Here we see God making a move to bring the gospel across the sea to the west.

In all these occasions reported in Acts, God spoke to people who were not looking for leading, not specifically trying to find God's will. He spoke at times when He desired a major change in the church's direction. And when He spoke He did not give His hearers a holy hunch or some kind of inner feeling. It was an unambiguous divine voice. The human hearers had no doubt that this angelic visitor was giving them specific verbal revelation. It was as clear and definite as a call on the telephone.

Don't misunderstand me here. Feelings are important. If we have a feeling, an impression, or a hunch, we ought to take that into careful consideration. But we ought not label such experiences the inerrant voice of the eternal God. Such experiences are not, at least in the biblical sense, divine revelation.

Sometimes hunches are worth heeding, particularly if they're all we have to go on. But I prefer the hunches of an experienced person because they have background that helps plant their hunches in reality. Informed hunches may be helpful, but it is close to blasphemy to raise inner impressions to the level of God's special revelation.

Decision-Making the Apostles' Way

Many people look back at the first century as a time of unique spiritual unity between God and man. Some see God mysteriously directing each action of the early believers and their congregations.

But when we look at most of the decisions the apostles made, we find a surprising thing; they made decisions the way we make them. They looked at their circumstances and came up with the best solution available.

For example, when it came to serving the Greek widows in the Aramaic community of Jerusalem, as we saw in chapter seven, they made a wise decision. Based on their ministry, on their gifts, and on what would help those widows most, they had the church elect men to take care of that responsibility. The apostles made a wise choice without any angelic guidance.

The early church leaders faced a crisis when the issue of circumcision divided Jewish and Gentile believers. So the church called a council at Jerusalem. There they looked at their circumstances, at their experiences, and studied Scripture. After plenty of discussion they came up with their decision: Gentiles are not subject to Jewish law (see Acts 15:1–31). Again, there was no special revelation. The council weighed the factors and made its choice.

As a brief footnote to our discussion of the apostles' decision-making processes, it is interesting to note that God guided New Testament believers in personal decisions only when such decisions related to the ministry of the gospel. As far as we know, Peter didn't get any special guidance from God when he wanted to buy a house or a horse. Nor do we hear of divine guidance when it came to decisions concerning marriage. In the New Testament, God's special revelation and guidance always had to do with ministry and the moving of God in the world.

When Revelation Comes

As we said earlier, God can do whatever He wants. If He chooses, He can give personal guidance. So if we feel God has blessed us with a personal revelation, here are two things to keep in mind.

First, special revelation cannot be contrary to God's moral will. I'm amazed at how often over the years I have had people tell me that, in their case, God gave them the right to do what He did not give other Christians permission to do.

Imagine a young man who wants to marry a non-Christian. He explains that his situation is an exception to God's rule. "I really have this deep sense that God has spoken to me, and that we are to marry each other." This young man has not heard the voice of God. God does not speak contrary to His Word. It's disobedient to attribute God's approval to actions that contradict His moral will as revealed in the Bible.

Second, if we think we have received divine revelation, and not just a hunch raised to the level of voice, we had better be sure that the voice we heard was indeed the voice of God. Not all angelic visitors come from heaven. Not all spirits are God's Spirit.

Take, for example, Edgar Cayce. Cayce, who is known to his followers as the "sleeping prophet," began as a Sunday school teacher. But over the years, his spiritist "readings" on the truth of God began to seriously disagree with God's revelation at all major points. According to Cayce's official biography *(The Story of Edgar Cayce: There Is a River* by Thomas Sugre, Dell, 1967), the sleeping prophet had doubts about the heretical teachings that began to pop up in the readings, but his mother reassured him, saying, "The devil cannot speak through a righteous man." But God's Word declares that none are righteous except Christ, who Himself was tempted by a visitation from Satan in the desert.

Jesus warns us in the Sermon on the Mount about a casual approach to our ministry:

"Not everyone who says to me, 'Lord, Lord,' will enter the kingdom of heaven, but only he who does the will of my Father who is in heaven. Many will say to me on that day, 'Lord, Lord, did we not prophesy in your name, and in your name drive out demons and perform many miracles?' Then I will tell them plainly, 'I never knew you. Away from me, you evildoers!' " (Matthew 7:21–23)

The fact that somebody is leading an apparently successful miracle crusade does not mean that this person is speaking from God. We must test the spirits as we make our choices.

11

General Principles

A second-best decision, diligently pursued, will often beat a first-best decision that is not diligently pursued.

The Bible contains God's wisdom on the best ways for us to make decisions about the big and small things that confront us every day. But I would also like to suggest four things that I have learned along the way as I have made decisions, watched others make them, and discovered the consequences. As far as I know, they do not come from the Scriptures. They are sheer Robinson, so take them for what they are worth. I know I have found them helpful, and it's on that basis that I recommend them.

Avoid Moods

One principle I have found helpful to me is this: As much as you can, avoid making a decision in a mood.

I find that moods have a way of distorting judgment. If I'm in an elevated mood, feeling unusually happy and positive, I tend to underestimate the difficulty of a task or project. As a result, I'm more likely to make a commitment without really examining the downside risks.

If I'm in a down mood, I'm more likely to overestimate difficulties and tend, therefore, to respond to opportunities negatively. So I try, as much as possible, to avoid making decisions when particularly moody.

This principle has special application for people who are going through grief. As a rule of thumb, having gone through a grief experience, one ought not to make any major decision, if at all possible, for at least six or seven months. Again and again, I have seen grieving people move to a new location, or enter into a new relationship, and then regret the consequences. They are often decisions based on a mood. Grief distorts judgment.

Mood swings are a part of life, but they don't make a healthy breeding ground for good decisions.

Separating Facts from Problems

A second principle of decision-making that has been helpful to me is to separate the facts of life from the problems before I make a decision.

For example, it may be a fact of life that you are five-foot-two. On the other hand, a problem is that you weigh two-hundred-fifty pounds. You can't do anything about the fact that you are five-foot-two, but you can do something about being overweight, unless a physical condition prohibits it.

The Army teaches a similar principle: Don't fight the problem, fight the enemy. If the enemy has five thousand troops and we have twenty-five hundred troops, a general can spend a lot of time wishing that he had five thousand troops, or wishing the enemy had only twenty-five hundred. But all that wishing can sap energy for battle. But if we're fighting the enemy, and we realize he outnumbers us two to one, then we have to decide whether we are going to commit ourselves to the struggle and how.

I've discovered that often, as we look at problems and questions, we waste a great deal of emotional energy trying to change the facts of life. Even though it's not as easy as it seems, we need to separate the facts of life from the problems.

Go for It!

A third principle worth mentioning is that a second-best decision, diligently pursued, will beat a first-best decision lackadaisically pursued.

Although we would like to live a life of total certainty, in making most of our decisions, we are seldom 100 percent certain—or even 95 percent certain. We know that lying is wrong, and so is adultery. Those decisions are relatively easy to make, though the consequences may be hard to bear.

But most decisions that don't have strong moral implications are 55/45 decisions. The difficulty often comes after having made the decision. Sometimes, just a week after making a decision, we may feel that we have chosen the 45 side instead of the 55 side. We can take comfort in this: If we pursue our decision vigorously, we may still beat out the better option. In fact, this is often the advantage of people who are convinced that God has led them into a particular activity. They usually give themselves to that activity wholeheartedly. The thing that wins is the determination, not necessarily that they have had specific divine guidance.

I picked up this principle from former Dallas Cowboys football coach, Tom Landry, who was a successful leader. The one thing a team cannot do when it gets into the huddle is to second-guess the quarterback. If the tackle or guard has decided that the best play is a long pass to the end zone, but the quarterback calls an end run, it may be that the end run is a second-best decision. But if the linemen start second-guessing and opposing the quarterback's decisions, everything comes apart. If the team executes the end run play, they have a better chance of gaining yardage than if they merely hope for a long pass and don't diligently pursue it.

The pursuit of the decision may be more important than the decision itself. Whatever we give ourselves to do, we've got to do it wholeheartedly. We shouldn't let ambivalence weaken the choices we've made. Instead, we need to forge ahead, and use what we've learned about our decision the next time we face a close call.

Set a Time Limit

I've also discovered that it is often best to set a time for making a decision.

Some folks are always looking for more facts. Of course there is a time and place for gathering facts to help us make a better decision, but decisions often must be made before we arrive at scientific certainty.

I've noticed that some of us find it extremely difficult to make a decision short of certainty, and therefore, don't make a decision at all. We must realize that to fail to make a decision is itself a decision.

Certain personality types seem to have a greater need for excessive information. In fact, textbooks on administration point out that seeking information is sometimes merely seeking relief from the responsibility of making decisions. In those cases, someone has to step in, assess that data, make the decision, and go with it.

Let's admit it: decision-making isn't always fun. Often it saps our energy. But indecision saps our energy as well.

So what I try to do as I look at a particular decision is this: If it's not a moral decision or one that has clear-cut biblical principles—if it's a choice between one good path and another good path—I decide to make the decision at an appointed time, and make the decision the information points to. Then I go with it. And I don't look back. I don't start daydreaming the next day, saying, "Maybe if I'd gone the other way, that would have been better after all." Such indecision may indicate the decision wasn't really made firmly.

12

Decision Danger Zones

When a decision looks good from several different perspectives, it is usually your best decision.

We have been making decisions since the time we decided to spit out our spinach. Although we have gotten through school, taken a job, dated, and then married, most of us have never had a moment's coaching on how to make decisions.

We're like ministers who are "natural-born preachers." They grew up talking, and they feel comfortable in front of a group. Yet they've never taken a course on homiletics—the principles of communication applied to preaching. Some sermons are effective and some are not; aside from attributing the differences to the Holy Spirit they don't know why one works and another doesn't.

People who teach homiletics study preachers and sermons. They try to answer questions such as, "What do you think about when you prepare to speak?" Or, "What goes on in a listener's head when she listens?" By analyzing the way effective preachers communicate, teachers of preaching learn what goes into strong introductions, smooth transitions, and effective conclusions.

The best preaching coaches know that untrained speakers often make some basic mistakes when they preach. For example, their introductions don't create a need to listen. Or their stories don't really illustrate their points. Or they lack a clear central idea. Self-taught preachers may speak well without training, but they will usually be more effective if they can be aware of the common mistakes that plague untrained speakers.

Like self-taught preachers, most of us are self-taught decision-makers. But recently, researchers have taken a close look at the way most of us make decisions. They have analyzed the way we make our choices in much the same way that a speaking coach analyzes introductions, outlines, conclusions, and delivery.

These researchers have sorted through the decision-making process and have discerned the most common mistakes most of us make when making choices. Obviously if we can spot our mistakes, we have a better chance of avoiding them.

Here are some of the most dangerous traps we stumble into. I call them the decision danger zones. And I've also provided a suggestion or two that can help us to avoid them.

Not Knowing Where You're Going

One of the biggest decision dangers is beginning without deciding where you want to go or how to get there. I have some friends who take their vacations by just taking off. They travel in a general direction to "see where it will take them." They resemble Christopher Columbus, who when he started out didn't know where he was going, when he got there didn't know where he was, and when he got back home didn't know where he had been.

Vacationing without a destination works out for travelers with a carefree, adventurous spirit, but it doesn't work well for those who want to get from A to Z in the most efficient manner. When we make decisions we should take some time to ask what we really want to decide, and then to consider what is the best way to make the decisions.

To know where you're going, make sure some of these obvious questions are not overlooked:

1. What exactly is the decision I have to make?
2. How should a decision like this one be made?
3. Should I involve other people?
4. How important is this decision anyhow?
5. Do I have to make this decision now?
6. Do I have to make this decision at all?
7. Do I need other perspectives to balance my biases or limitations?

Take an hour or so to write out your answers to these basic questions. You'll be surprised at what you may have overlooked, and you'll be pleased at how your decision will gain definition.

Answering the Wrong Question

Often we are tempted to ask the questions that are easily answered rather than the harder, more crucial questions. For example, it is simpler to ask if I should marry Andy rather than to ask if I should get married at all. Or if I should get married now.

We sometimes get caught up in the emotion of secondary decisions and ignore the broader, more essential issues in the larger decisions. When high-school students think about college they usually examine catalogs or visit different campuses. They are concerned about the cost of tuition or where the school is located. They may never stop to ask a bigger question, "Should I go to college at all?" Or, "What exactly am I looking for in a college?" Or, "What do I expect a college education to do for me?" Or, "What do I want to do with my life?" Some Christians look only at Christian colleges or Bible schools without asking a more basic question of why they are investing in a college education at all.

A young Christian woman who plans to enter medicine as a career must first ask hard questions about a school's science department, as well as the percentage of the college's graduates who are accepted into medical school. Only when those questions are answered should other factors such as tuition, Christian commitment, or location be considered.

This whole danger zone of answering the wrong question forces us to go back to an issue we discussed earlier in the book. Namely, if you ask, "How can I know the will of God in this decision?" then you may approach the issue with your mind set on signs or impressions. You place yourself in a vulnerable position where you are susceptible to the influence of coincidences.

On the other hand, if you frame your question, "How can I make a wise decision that honors God?" you ask a question that focuses on the process.

How you frame your question, therefore, determines the information and advice you will seek. It's important to ask, "Does my question really fit the problem?" Or, "Are there other ways to frame it?" If you state your question in several different ways, each new frame may throw new light on your decision.

Let's be specific and show how different ways of framing a question can lead to different answers and different ways of seeing the whole problem.

A family that has just moved into a new community might ask several different questions when deciding which church to join. Look at several different "frames," or questions, through which this family might view their situation.

- *What is the denomination of the church?*

  If they have come from a strong denominational background they may limit their choice to a brand name they know. Cultural norms and familiar worship patterns will be strong elements in their choice.

- *What essential doctrines does the church believe or not believe?*

  This way of framing the question puts the emphasis on the beliefs of the congregation more than on its style of worship or its denomination.

- *Will our children be happy in the church we join?*

  With this frame, the youth program of the congregation takes on stronger significance for the family.

- *How far do we travel to get to the church?*

  The strongest church may be twenty miles away, while a less attractive church may be right down the street. How important will distance be in fitting into the congregation or having the children participate? What would bring you closer to the Lord on Sunday morning: packing the family into the car and driving to the big church across town, or walking together to the smaller church down the street?

- *Where can we best serve Jesus Christ with our gifts and abilities?*

  This completely different frame might motivate a family to join a church in the inner city or become part of a smaller body where needs are greater and they can play a strategic role in the life of the congregation.

No particular frame is any better or worse than any other. But the lesson is obvious. When a decision looks good through several different frames, it is usually your best decision.

Be Sure of What You Don't Know

Still another decision danger zone you might face is being sure of what you really don't know. If you are overconfident of your own judgments or opinions, you may not gather the information needed to make a good decision.

Many years ago, a growing congregation in the center of a large city had the opportunity to purchase land near the church for parking. The church board knew that many of the people came to the services by bus and trolley, and sufficient on-street parking existed for those who came by car. Since this was "common knowledge," the elders decided not to buy land for parking but instead to give a large amount of money to a missions project.

What they did not bother to find out was whether buses and trolleys would continue to serve the central city on Sundays. Had they taken time to talk with the transit authority officials, they would have discovered that fewer and fewer people were using the bus or trolley on weekends. What is more, the transit board was already considering a drastic cut in its Sunday bus and trolley service.

A few years after the decision not to purchase land, the bus service to the central city was cut. More people were then forced to drive to the church, but when they got downtown they could not find a place to park. As a result, the church lost members. And at this point the land for parking was no longer available.

If only the board members had asked themselves, "What don't we know?" "What information do we need?" "How can we obtain it?" Then they might have made a different decision that would have better served the ongoing ministry of their church.

Avoiding Disagreement

One decision danger zone we sometimes fall into is surrounding ourselves with "yes men" and "yes women." In other words, our decisions sometimes fail because when we are sure we are right, we refuse to listen to someone who thinks we are wrong.

For many years Alfred P. Sloan led the powerful General Motors Corporation. Once after the board made an important decision, Sloan said, "Gentlemen, I take it we are all in complete agreement on the decision here. So I propose we postpone the decision until our next meeting to give ourselves time to develop some disagreement and perhaps gain some understanding of what the decision is all about" *(Decision Traps* by J. Edward Russo and Paul J. Schoemaker, Simon and Schuster).

Dissent keeps you from believing you are infallible. Pastors who feel comfortable with only church board members who admire them and are overly concerned with pleasing them may not be well served when it comes to decision-making.

People who are free to disagree put alternatives before the group that minimize the risks inherent in every important decision. Dissenters help us see the unforeseen negative consequences that may be invisible to us because of our happy unanimity.

Loyalty to a group does not mean that we go along to get along. It means that we state our viewpoint openly and clearly. The responsibility falls on leaders to create the environment for this kind of freewheeling honesty. Disagreement forces us to check our facts and state the basis for our decision.

But then, when a decision is made, loyalty requires all members of the group to do everything possible to make the decision succeed.

A growing church needed more space for the crowds that were attending. The board met to vote on a $10-million-dollar building program for an auditorium that would seat four thousand people. One of the leaders raised an obvious question, "What would happen if our pastor was hit by a car and we had to replace him next year?"

What would happen indeed? With that simple question the board had to face the reality that many of the people who attended the church came because of the personal charisma of their strong pastor. Thus the board decided to put off the building project, and instead invested funds toward strengthening the ministries of the church that would serve the congregation even if their pastor left.

Disagreement does not mean that God is not working. Unanimity is not unity. Dissent can stir the imagination and force us to consider uncertainties in the decision-making process.

Using Yesterday's Battle Plans

Generals learn to fight wars by studying battles of the past. The British did that when they fought against the colonists in the Revolutionary War, and they lost. The generals in the South and North in the American Civil War did that; their weapons went beyond their knowledge, and there was needless carnage. Saddam Hussein did that when he challenged the Allied forces over his occupation of Kuwait. He believed that the tactics that had served him well in a war with Iran would work in a war against the United States and coalition forces. As a result he committed a third-rate army to fight against the mightiest war machine in history. While we can learn from the past, we cannot occupy the past. The present is not the past, even though it might look the same.

We sometimes develop "rules of thumb" that worked in the past and—we assume—will continue to work in the future. But we constantly need to ask ourselves whether or not on some Tuesday when we weren't looking, the world in which we developed our rules of thumb drastically changed.

The seven last words of a dying church are usually, "We've never done it that way before." Often we come to believe that our own personal approaches to life or ministry are as inspired and permanent as the Bible. They are not.

In the 1950s, churches grew by emphasizing the Sunday school. But that is seldom true today. Body life services that worked well in the 1960s have much less appeal in the 1990s. Evangelistic visitation brought scores of men and women to Christ in the 1970s, but the un-welcome mat is out in front of most houses in many communities today.

Bishop Henry Lyte's famous hymn "Abide with Me" goes a bit overboard with the words, "Change and decay in all around I see." Change doesn't necessarily mean moral rot, but it does demand that we consider new strategies and new campaigns to bring newcomers into the church. We need to grab hold of the flame and not the ashes from the altars of the past.

Assuming Group Infallibility

Some research indicates that if all things are equal, which they seldom are, a group makes better decisions than an individual. Proverbs 15:22 warns, "Plans fail for lack of counsel, but with many advisers they succeed." What the proverb does not say is that success depends on the quality of the advisers.

One informed person who knows what he or she is talking about beats group ignorance anytime. A group works well only if the members are qualified, and if they are allowed to think for themselves.

Even experts disagree. Worse yet, experts in a group will sometimes agree for the wrong reasons, or they will agree prematurely on the wrong solution. They may reinforce one another so that the group feels certain they have made a wise decision when they have not.

Respect and friendship within a group increases the likelihood that it will make poor decisions. A well-known example of the dangers of this unhealthy group orientation took place during the John F. Kennedy administration. A faulty decision caused the defeat of American forces in the invasion of Cuba at the Bay of Pigs, resulting in embarrassment for the president and the nation.

President Kennedy had surrounded himself with a committee of some of the shrewdest advisers in the country. The reason that this group of experts made a poor decision was not their low IQs. They failed because they wanted to be liked by others in the group. They allowed friendship and loyalty to overwhelm their decision-making process.

Advisers who were tempted to speak up in opposition to the attack decided against it out of fear of being disliked, or because they didn't want to waste everyone's time. In a memorandum written before the committee assembled, Arthur Schlesinger, one of the members of the Kennedy inner circle, acknowledged that he considered the invasion of Cuba a mistake. But he kept silent during the discussion. Robert Kennedy, the president's brother and the U.S. attorney general, had cornered Schlesinger after discovering that he opposed the invasion. Kennedy had put it bluntly, "Arthur, you may be right or you may be wrong, but the president has made up his mind. Don't push any further." So Schlesinger kept quiet. The environment wasn't right for voicing dissent.

Irving Janis, a Yale university professor, studied this incident and others like it, and came up with the idea of "Groupthink" (*Groupthink,* 2nd ed., Houghton Mifflin, 1982). Janis singled out four factors in a group that can lead to disaster.

1. *Cohesiveness.* The members of the group know and like each other and want to preserve harmony. Disagreement is stifled.
2. *Insulation.* The group makes its decisions in isolation and cannot—or will not—discuss its conclusions with outsiders.
3. *High stress.* The importance of the decision, its complexity, or a tight deadline puts group members under heavy pressure. They rush toward a decision but ignore important information.
4. *Strong directive leadership.* A group usually wants to please its leader. Bad decisions often come when the head of the group states clearly and forcefully what she or he favors.

"Groupthink" has probably been responsible for a number of our country's most embarrassing moments. Take, for example, the United States' ignoring all warning signs before the Japanese bombed Pearl Harbor.

More recent administrations have brought onto the White House staff, friends or ideological soulmates of the president. While we don't know all that went on in decisions that were made, it is evident that there were folks who "went along to get along" and bad policy was made.

Some say "Groupthink" contributed to the United States' defeat in the Vietnam War. Scholars seem to agree that "Groupthink" propelled the Watergate scandal during the Nixon administration. Or what about GM's development of the Corvair—that unique car that went nowhere?

"Groupthink" also explains many of the decisions made at churches, mission agencies, and seminaries by groups of devoted, intelligent men and women who got together and just happened to come out with some incredibly bad choices.

Not all "Groupthink" is bad, of course. Sometimes consensus is more important than debate. A football team huddles to get the play straight and then executes it together. In important and complex decisions, though, groups and their leaders must guard against conformity. Quick decisions made without serious debate or pressured by group overconfidence can lead to disaster.

America's Supreme Court has an interesting custom. The newest member of the court speaks his or her mind on a decision first. Then the next-newest speaks. This continues until all of the members have spoken; then the Chief Justice speaks last. In that way, no one is held back by fear of differing with the opinion of a more experienced judge. This wouldn't be a bad idea for most of our churches or business committees to follow.

Avoid "Groupthink." Encourage every member of your decision-making group to speak. Learn to value dissent.

Misreading the Lessons of Experience

Experience is a great teacher, but sometimes during our sessions in the school of experience we learn too much. People with long track records can be invaluable when you have a decision to make. They can offer sound counsel that comes out of experience. It's important, however, to evaluate their counsel. After all, you and no one else are responsible for your decisions.

You must ask how much another person's experience qualifies him to counsel you, and if he is the only person you should consult. Don't stop with just one bit of experienced, sage advice. Find out if others with similar experiences reached different conclusions.

Assuming That Decisions Stay Made

It feels good to make a decision, especially if it proves to be a good one. All the anxiety and uncertainty are gone, and a calm confidence takes over.

But that confidence can lead us to another decision danger zone, and that's the assumption that once a decision is made, it stays made.

Decisions—like beds—sometimes get unmade. All of our decisions are based on assumptions about ourselves, our situation, our world. It is important to try to state the assumptions behind our important decisions. If what we assumed as a basis for decision turns out to be inaccurate, then we need to reexamine our decision.

In the early 1980s Denver, Colorado was a boom town. It was the oil capital of the United States. Office buildings were erected, apartment complexes went up, and housing in the community was scarce. The housing that was available was very expensive.

In this context, the trustees of Denver Seminary decided to build new apartments for its student families, to provide these students and their loved ones with affordable housing. Plans were drawn up. A campaign to raise funds was started. Then oil prices plunged and Denver's economy went bust. Soon, inexpensive housing in the city became available again.

Since the decision to construct apartments had been made because living quarters in the city were scarce and expensive, the trustees reversed their vote to build, even though they had already invested a significant amount of energy and money in the project. The assumptions had changed, and therefore their decision had to be changed.

The world is constantly changing, and sometimes that means that the decisions we made last year become unmade. Don't fall into the trap of believing that all decisions are irreversible.

Believing in Feeling

Some people who are otherwise fairly rational seem to change when it comes to making decisions. Suddenly they seem to believe that intuition is better than a systematic procedure.

Most of us make our choices intuitively. Intuition works well for small, unimportant decisions. For example, some decisions may not demand much systematic thought:

what to have for dinner, whether or not to visit a friend next weekend, or what color to paint the dining room.

But in larger decisions where more is at stake, feelings are dangerous business. Our intuitions are colored not only by the facts of the matter, but also by complicated factors such as anxiety, fatigue, frustration, boredom, a letter from the IRS telling you that you will be audited, or perhaps even by what you had for dinner last night!

A series of studies in the medical field demonstrate the unreliability of intuition. Radiologists who make diagnoses from X rays or doctors who decide that children need to have their tonsils out show far less unanimity than physicians suspect. In fact, a wise patient who is facing surgery asks for a second or third opinion before agreeing to an operation.

Of course, intuition is part of God's design of us all, and it forms an essential part of all decision-making. You use it when you frame an issue, state your position, or look for information.

But whenever you are making a crucial choice, a systematic process for making the decision will usually produce better results than intuition.

One simple systematic approach is to list the advantages and disadvantages of a particular choice on a piece of paper. Assign a value from one to five for each "pro" and "con," and then choose the alternative with the highest score. A thoughtful approach to your decision usually beats your best hunches.

Good decisions are no harder to make than poor ones if we stop and think about them in a systematic way. And good decisions are far easier to live with.

Closing Thoughts on Open Minds

Dr. Erich Klinger at the University of Minnesota conducted a study several years ago in which he determined that all of us face between three hundred and seventeen thousand decisions every day.

While an open mind is commendable, it is commendable only when its owner has the courage to make a decision. That courage then clears the mind for action after all sides of a question have been considered.

None of us is perfect, and not all of our decisions will be good ones. But if you get into the habit of making decisions and acting on them, experience will help you develop your judgment. It is better to be right fifty percent of the time and get something done than it is to get nothing done because you are afraid to be wrong.

Former President Ronald Reagan said he learned the importance of decision-making early in life. An aunt had taken him to a cobbler to have a pair of shoes made for him. The shoemaker asked young Ronald Reagan, "Do you want a square toe or a round toe?"

Reagan hemmed and hawed. So the cobbler said, "Come back in a day or two and let me know what you want."

A few days later the shoemaker saw Reagan on the street and asked what he had decided about the shoes. "I still haven't made up my mind," the boy answered. "Very well," said the cobbler.

When Reagan received the shoes he was shocked to see that one shoe had a square toe and the other a round toe.

"Looking at those shoes every day taught me a lesson," said Reagan, years later. "If you don't make your own decisions, somebody else will make them for you!"

The sovereign God has made us people, not puppets. We have His Word to guide us, His love to redeem us, and His assurance to make us capable to make choice choices.

Note to the Reader

The publisher invites you to share your response to the message of this book by writing Discovery House Publishers, Box 3566, Grand Rapids, MI 49501, USA. For information about other Discovery House books, music, or videos, contact us at the same address or call 1-800-653-8333. Find us on the Internet at http://www.dhp.org/ or send e-mail to books@dhp.org.